S0-FAH-937

Intentional Responsive Adult Practices

Supporting Kids to Not Only Overcome Adversity but to Thrive

ERIK K. LAURSEN, PHD

ISBN: 978-1-4834-8622-2 (sc)
ISBN: 978-1-4834-8621-5 (e)

Library of Congress Control Number: 2018906326

Lulu Publishing Services rev. date: 06/28/2018

Contents

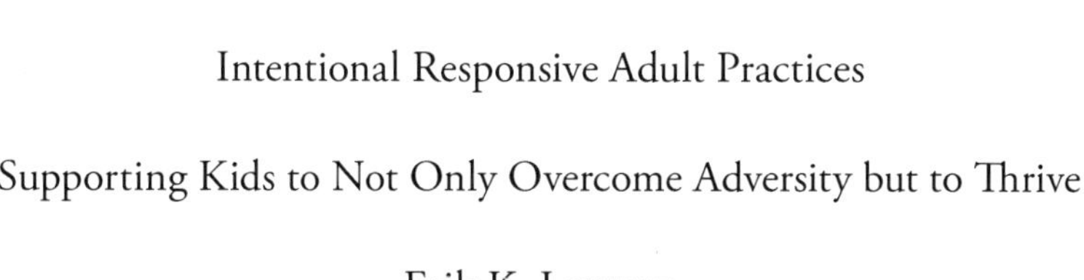

Intentional Responsive Adult Practices

Supporting Kids to Not Only Overcome Adversity but to Thrive

Erik K. Laursen

About the Author

Erik K. Laursen, PhD, is an internationally recognized developer of innovative programs for high-risk children and families. He has created therapeutic treatment programs in private residential, educational, and foster care organizations; therapeutic services in public schools; and services for children with neurological differences. Dr. Laursen has authored more than two dozen publications and has served on the editorial boards of the journals *Reclaiming Children and Youth* and *Families in Society.* He has served as a board officer of the Virginia Association of Specialized Education Facilities and as president of Strengths Based Services International. Erik is the recipient of the Spirit of Crazy Horse award, My Brother's Keeper award, the Spotlight on Excellence award, and the University of Richmond Innovations in Teaching award.

Erik earned a MEd in special education and a PhD in urban services from Virginia Commonwealth University, where he taught organizational culture, qualitative research, and ethics for ten years. Currently, he is an adjunct associate professor at the University of Richmond and trains youth practitioners worldwide. He has developed and codeveloped several courses, including Cultures of Respect and Trauma Informed Foster Care.

Erik served UMFS in Richmond, Virginia, for thirty years, last as the executive director of Charterhouse School and vice president of research and development. Among the highlights of his career are a sixty-five thousand miles motorcycle journey across the United States with twelve high-risk youth, a wagon train across Denmark, and a two-masted sailboat journey on the European rivers. In recent years, his passion led to advocacy for older children in foster care and supporting and helping young people with neurological differences to transition from high school to college.

On a personal level, Erik enjoys spending time with his wife, traveling, bicycling, and exploring art and culture. Both being from Denmark, they spend much of the summer maintaining and strengthening their cultural roots and relations with their families there. During the rest of the year, they indulge in experiences with their two children and friends in the United States. Erik's signature strengths are love, perseverance, perspective, creativity, and fairness.

Praise for the Book

"Ready to help kids who are in need? Dr. Erik Laursen's book, *Intentional Responsive Adult Practices*, should be required reading for anyone working with at-risk youth or youth who've experienced adverse childhood experiences. Dr. Laursen engages you with essential research findings, key insights, reflections, and activities. By the end of the book, you will feel better equipped for an exciting journey in helping children who need it most."

—Ryan M. Niemiec, PsyD, author of *Character Strengths Interventions: A Field Guide for Practitioners* and *Mindfulness and Character Strengths*; education director and psychologist of the global nonprofit VIA Institute on Character

"As a developmental psychologist, therapeutic director and researcher of resilient development, I consider Dr. Laursen's new book the next critical text for training of youth-care leaders and youth-care practitioners. His integration of brain science, developmental needs and strength-based approaches are thorough yet easily understood and applicable. Dr. Laursen's decades of application, leadership, and research in caring for youth with adverse experiences have culminated in this educational manual filled with examples, resources, and practices that have the capacity to change a care culture from *survive* to *thrive*—for the youth in care, the leaders, and the practitioners!"

—Tara Devine, PhD, codirector of Integral Flow in Houston, Texas

"This book is a must-read for anyone who works with or who cares for or about children and youth, particularly those children whose lives have been made more challenging by circumstances beyond their control. Laursen adopts a positive tone, and his examples, drawn from his extensive experience, reflect his deep respect and hope for the lives he is working to change. He also incorporates a diverse, multicultural perspective. Based on a solid research foundation, Laursen provides a range of practical strategies that will be useful to teachers, mental health workers, and numerous other professions that touch the lives of children and youth."

—Fred Orlove, PhD; co-chair, Trauma Informed Schools Committee, Greater Richmond SCAN; and professor emeritus of Special Education and Disability Policy, Virginia Commonwealth University

"Laursen artfully takes the reader on a journey that blends essential science with responsive and 'intentional' practice. This refreshing and comprehensive book provides those working with challenging young people a framework that encourages a strengths-based perspective and a dedicated focus on positive outcomes! An absolute must-read for the frontline practitioner."

—Paul W. Baker, PhD, director of Clinical Services, Allambi Care, Warners Bay, NSW, Australia; and developer of the PersonBrain Model

"School administrators repeatedly ask for training to help their teachers, counselors, and themselves to better work with children who have experienced adversity and trauma. This book is a direct response to their needs. It provides easy-to-understand explanations of the effects of trauma and strengths-based strategies to help educators respond to children's needs. The book and the accompanying course is a go-to resource for professional learning communities and an essential guide for educators and school administrators!"

—Laura Kuti, PhD; assistant chair, Graduate Education, Curriculum & Instruction, University of Richmond

Foreword

Several years ago, I traveled to virtually the other side of the world and met Erik K. Laursen in the Black Hills of South Dakota for a gathering with hundreds of Circle of Courage folk. Erik's stories instantly made an indelible impression on me. His adventures with young people reverberated with relevance, truth, and innovation. I returned to the South Pacific and retold these tales until Erik could visit and tell the stories personally, along with his wife, Jannie, and a couple of other friends.

Erik's stories are memorable because they're inherently strengths-based. It is a delicate craft to describe the work we do with young people. Sure, stakeholders need to know their investments are reaching the most deserving youth, but the temptation is to write reports that inadvertently demean young people and their families. In this refreshing book, Erik has found a way to honestly and succinctly capture the real pain, difficulty, or vulnerability many young people experience, while prioritizing and maintaining their dignity in the process. Here we witness a relocation of power in favor of those who are most marginalized.

This is dichotomous work. Strengths-based approaches with young people demand that practitioners balance opposing tensions to discover a healthy whole. We're consciously choosing to focus on *strength* more than *weakness.* We see *solutions* and not just *problems.* As this book encourages us, we can daydream about *possibilities* rather than *punishment.* We *dialogue* more than we *diagnose.* We're committed to *care* more than *cure.* Erik regularly reminds us to shift from *pain* toward *hope.* You get the idea; it's a flipped script.

While the core concepts may seem simple, Erik's gathered a vast collection of compelling evidence. He's somehow made neuroscience appetizing, digestible, and irresistible—you'll be craving brains! This book consolidates and distils pertinent philosophies and integrates into readily applicable and practical approaches for and with young people. The bibliography here feels like a map for future treasure hunts, and Erik even offers "explorations" at the end of each chapter, suggesting strengths-based practice is a continual commitment. Erik clearly practices what he preaches, role modeling the humility and grace we all need to work effectively with young people.

I sincerely hope you devour and enjoy this book as much as I did. I'm certain this is a book you'll read more than once and lend to friends. Flip your work, and have fun doing so. I'm sure you'll discover a few stories of your own that may even travel to the other side of the world.

Rod Baxter

Korowai Tupu, youth worker

Wellington, Aotearoa, New Zealand

Preface

Intentional Responsive Adult Practices (*i*RAP) grew out of my work and passion for children and youth to achieve well-being and success in life. Young people who grow up with adversity and chronic, unpredictable, and unresolved stress have a special place in my heart. To fulfill their life dreams, they need to be wrapped with support from caring, understanding, and warm adults. I have worked with children and their families for more than forty years in residential treatment, special education, foster care, community-based services, and crisis stabilization and with young people with neurological differences.

Trained as a teacher, I have always believed that it is my responsibility to create experiences that help young people learn and grow. High risk youth have amazed me again and again with their ingenuity, creativity, persistence, and stubbornness. I learned early on to always begin with and focus on what's *strong*, not what's *wrong* with children and youth. This approach creates hope and opens doors for new possibilities.

I wrote the book to support and honor adults who work with young people and their families in communities, schools, group homes, treatment facilities, and the juvenile justice system. I use the name "youth practitioner" throughout the book to collectively refer to people who commit their lives to serving and supporting high-risk children and youth in their respective fields, whether they are teachers, counselors, youth workers, mentors, coaches, social workers, police officers, correctional officers, or mental health workers. The book is written for practitioners to provide them with knowledge and practical strategies to support young people in fulfilling their aspirations.

Numerous books, articles, and courses present knowledge and research documenting the effects of growing up with trauma and the long-term behavioral, intellectual, social, and health consequences of these experiences. It is important to know about these effects, but knowledge alone does not help children thrive. Helping kids overcome adversity and thrive is the result of intentional responsive adult practices or *i*RAP. When adults learn to reflect and intentionally respond to children's pain, they can assist with the transformation of their lives.

Overview of the Book

In chapter 1, I present the beliefs and assumptions that undergird the rest of the book: a strengths-based paradigm, solution-focused practices, and positive psychology.

Chapter 2 describes how the fields of psychology, neuroscience, resilience, and positive youth development have converged in the identification of universal growth needs necessary for thriving. Five growth needs—belonging, achievement, autonomy, contribution, and hope and purpose—are explored in more detail.

Chapter 3 covers the essentials of normal brain development, with focus on understanding that a person's DNA provides the blueprint for development and that later experiences shape a person's brain architecture. I also highlight the *plasticity* of the brain, making it open to use and adapt to supportive experiences provided by positive adults, peers, and environments in its continued development.

In chapter 4, I present a case example of psychosocial pain based on the autobiography of Liz Murray. The persistent, unpredictable, and unresolved experiences set the foundation for understanding how adversity—or trauma—disrupts child and adolescent development.

Chapter 5 presents the findings of the groundbreaking adverse childhood experiences study. It's necessary for youth practitioners to understand that child abuse and neglect disrupts learning, self-regulation, and relationships and has dire health consequences. I also discuss how adverse community experiences contribute to disrupted development.

In chapter 6, I highlight how adverse childhood experiences and adverse community experiences may disrupt brain development. While these facts do not excuse young people's actions, they often propel youth practitioners to compassion and action. Equipped with the knowledge presented in chapters 5 and 6, youth practitioners may realize that kids cannot just decide to stop their self-defeating behaviors. Traditional approaches to discipline will typically increase their social and emotional dislocations. Instead, they need intentional responsive adult practices to find pathways out of self-defeating behaviors toward well-being and thriving.

The last four chapters of the book present ten intentional responsive adult practices to support kids to not only overcome adversity but to thrive.

Chapters 7, 8, 9, and 10 describe four intentional capacity-building practices designed to bolster young people's "immune systems." They are creating intentional relationships, developing character strengths, solidifying executive functions, and tapping into culture and faith. I chose to focus on these four capacity-building areas because young people who live with adversity have histories of relationship failure, feel they don't count, have poorly developed executive functions, and have lost connection to their culture and faith. Each chapter includes vignettes to illustrate the practical applications of each capacity.

In chapter 7, I provide practical steps to create intentional adult and peer relationships with adult-wary youth. As victims of the deficit approach, young people who have experienced adversity carry with them (and often identify with) one or more of the multiple diagnoses they have been assigned. Therefore, I highlight in chapter 8 the need to learn to focus on what's strong, not what's wrong, by naming and developing young people's character strengths. Chapter 9 focuses on solidifying executive functions because the development of these often is disrupted by toxic experiences. In chapter 10, I provide suggestions to reconnect young people with their culture and faith to develop and strengthen the essence of who they are.

Finally, in chapter 11, I present six intentional solution-finding practices to support young people during times of struggle or planning for their desired future. The practices can be used as crisis intervention, behavior support, co-creation of positive outcomes in the here and now, and to clarify young people's hopes for the future. The practices are Set Your Compass; Intentionality; Support; Engage; Empower; and Responsive Environments. Figure 1 provides a conceptual map for the book.

I hope the book is helpful to youth practitioners in many fields. It is also used in conjunction with a three-day professional development course of the same name and as a text in a three-credit graduate course I currently teach at the University of Richmond.

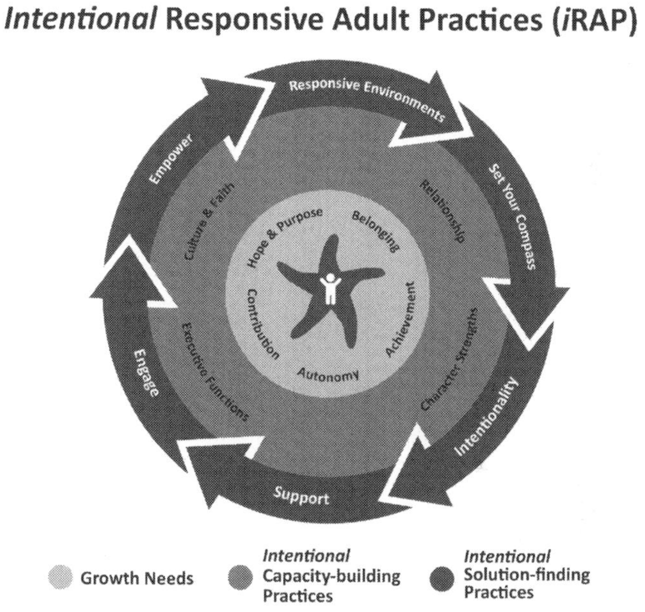

Intentional Responsive Adult Practices (_i_RAP)

Figure 1. Intentional Responsive Adult Practices

Stories

The book is full of stories about young people because we learn best from stories. All the stories in this book are true. Most of them are based on my own experiences, memories, notes, or recordings. Others have been shared with me by friends and colleagues, based on their experiences with young people. Some of these stories are based on interviews, and others are written collaboratively. In the end, my friends and colleagues reviewed the stories and gave me permission to use them. To assure anonymity, all names of children and youth have been changed, as has other identifying information, to protect their privacy. While the names of my friends and colleagues are their real names, they are only identified by the state and country where they live.

It is disturbing and unfortunate that the stories are true; that children have lived the lives the stories depict. It is my hope that readers can learn from the resilience of these young people and gain insight into the tremendous influence supportive youth practitioners had on their lives.

Acknowledgments

I am indebted to all the young people who have taught me to look beyond anger, verbal abuse, insults, or withdrawal. They have taught me to become a better listener, to ask questions, and to talk less. Many young people have let me into their inner worlds and shared their pain, struggles, and hopes for the future. I have learned the power of tapping into their strengths to find solutions, rather than telling them what to do. Most importantly, I have learned to partner and collaborate with young people, rather than acting as if I were an expert on their lives.

My experiences and insights have evolved with my soul mate and wife of forty-five years, Jannie. Our professional journeys have allowed us to reflect and share experiences since the early 1970s. She worked as a teacher, assistant principal, and principal in inner-city schools with 100 percent poverty in Richmond, Virginia, for almost thirty years, while I worked with high-risk youth in the private sector. Our experiences kindled daily reflections of what we could do differently or more of to help kids thrive. Her experiences and perspectives are interwoven throughout the book. Along the way, our children, Stine and Mikkel, have given us love, joy, worries, pride, challenges, insight, and a whole lot more; possibly best described as the most humbling and awesome experience of being parents. I am grateful for all they have taught me.

This project began in collaboration with Lesley du Toit, who brought forty years of experiences in child care protection, residential care and treatment, policy development, and transformation of systems for children. She led the transformation of the child and youth care system in South Africa for the Mandela government and later took on the role of deputy minister for the Ministry of Children and Family Development in British Columbia, Canada. After field-testing the project, we decided to refine and finish it individually to make it fit the primary audiences with which each of us works.

My work and the book would not have been possible without friends and colleagues, including Paul Baker, Rod Baxter, Howard Bath, Paul Brasler, Larry Brendtro, Melinda Bright, Martin Brokenleg, Jackie Cowan, Tara Devine, Brendan Folmar, Mark Freado, Howard Garner, George Giacobbe, Douglas Glick, Kristina Kallini, Laura Kuti, Rosemary Lambie, Lise Laursen, Nicholas Long, Courtney Mills, Vernon Oliver, Zandra Rawlinson, Tonya Salley-Goodwin, Neal Sarahan, Matthew Selekman, Steve van Bockern, and Sasha Yazdgerdi.

During the early development of the project, Lesley and I shared the information with audiences in Canada, Australia, the United States, and New Zealand. Special thanks to the School of Special Education Needs, Behaviour and Engagement in Perth, Western Australia; Allambi Care in Charlestown, New South Wales, Australia; and UMFS in Richmond, Virginia. These organizations trusted us to present the first versions of our ideas and gave us valuable feedback.

I appreciate the reviews and edits by Irene Walker-Bolton and Kate Cassada, along with on-the-spot comments, suggestions, and edits to the manuscript by several course participants. I am grateful to Kasia Borkowski, Meghan Ellis, Tricia Giles-Wang, Jamie Leech, Gregg Morris, Wade Puryear, Neal Sarahan, and Craig Simmons for sharing their stories.

PART I

Foundation of Intentional Responsive Adult Practices

1

Introduction

Most likely, you have heard this story before, but I find that it doesn't hurt to be reminded of it.[1] First let me tell you the story, and then I'll explain why I use it.

Once upon a time, there was a wise man who would go to the ocean to do his writing. He had a habit of walking on the beach before he began his work.

One day as he was walking along the shore, he saw—in the distance—a person moving like a dancer. He smiled to himself at the thought of someone who would dance to the day, and so he walked faster to catch up.

As he got closer, he noticed it was young man and that he was not dancing at all. The young man was reaching down to the shore, picking up small objects, and throwing them into the ocean.

He came closer and called out, "Good morning! May I ask what you are doing?"

The young man paused, looked up, and replied, "Throwing starfish into the ocean."

"Why are you throwing starfish into the ocean?" asked the somewhat startled wise man.

The young man replied, "The sun is up, and the tide is going out. If I don't throw them in, they'll die."

Upon hearing this, the wise man commented, "But, young man, do you not realize that there are miles and miles of beach and there are starfish all along every mile? You can't possibly make a difference!"

At this, the young man bent down, picked up yet another starfish, and threw it into the ocean. As it met the water, he said, "It made a difference for that one."

All of us have opportunities to make a difference in young people's lives, but sometimes we may ask ourselves how much of a difference we really can make. It may be true if we think of big issues, like ending child abuse and neglect, preventing poverty, or stopping community violence. But the thought often sneaks up on us and prevents us from making a difference where we can. We may not be able to change the big issues, but as youth practitioners, we can commit to making a difference in a child's life every day.

The book provides youth practitioners with knowledge and practical strategies—called intentional responsive adult practices (*i*RAP)—to support young people to grow and develop throughout childhood, adolescence, and into young adulthood. Regardless of the context in which young people grow up, they need safety, caring, the opportunity to learn, the ability to manage stress, and a strong sense of purpose. Their journey toward living a fulfilled life in community with others provides growth experiences that allow for a healthy integration of internal strengths and resources, drawn from their social ecology.

The world is filled with individual, family, community, and societal challenges. Increasing numbers of children are born into lives filled with adverse childhood experiences or adverse community environments. Some live with their parents' mental illness or substance abuse, while still others grow up witnessing violence in or outside of their home or experiencing some form of abuse. Many children are preoccupied with preparing for the next unpredictable event, constantly taxing their stress response system, rather than attending to normal developmental tasks. Without internal and external resources to cope with adversity, young people may develop social and emotional problems that become significant barriers to well-being.

Philosophy of Practice

The strategies outlined in the book enhance adult capacities to provide supportive ecologies and relationships where children and young people thrive. They create conditions that support young people in meeting psychosocial growth needs, achieve well-being, and pursue happiness. The book is centered within a strengths-based paradigm, solution-focused practices, and positive psychology.

Strengths-based practice is preoccupied with what is strong in people. It creates conditions that enable people to identify, value, and mobilize their strengths and capacities in the process of change.[2] Adults and youth bring their strengths and resources to their individual and shared journeys throughout life. The strengths approach is a sharp contrast to the more common deficit paradigm, which is based on faults, deficits, and disorders in people. The deficit approach uses a language of deficits—words such as *dis*order, *dis*ease, *dis*ruption, *dis*respect, *dis*obedience, and *dys*function.

Strengths-based practice begins with the belief that people do the best they can to cope with stress and challenges and that all people have strengths and capacities that can be nurtured to help overcome adversity.[3] This belief creates opportunities, hope, and solutions, rather than defeat and hopelessness. The strengths approach vests power in young people to develop resources and capacities. It changes the role of adults from experts, initiators, and directors to that of partners and collaborators.

Solution-focused practices originate from solution-focused therapy and are future-oriented.[7] These practices are goal-directed and emphasize solution finding, rather than finding problems, deficits, and faults. The core assumption of solution-focused practice is that people do not experience a problem all the time. Therefore, finding exceptions to a problem can lead to problem resolution.

Spotlight 1. Principles of Strengths-Based Practice

The Strengths Perspective in Social Work Practice:[4]

- Every individual, group, family, and community has strengths.
- Trauma and abuse, illness, and struggle may be injurious, but they also may be sources of challenge and opportunity.
- Assume that you do not know the upper limits of the capacity to growth and change, and take individual, group, and community aspirations seriously.
- We best serve clients by collaborating with them.
- Every environment is full of resources.
- Caring and caretaking are essential elements in all contexts.

The Strengths Approach[5]

- All people have strengths and capacities.
- People can change. Given the right conditions and resources, people's capacity to learn and grow can be harnessed and mobilized.
- People change and grow through their strengths and capacities.
- People are the experts on their own situations.
- The problem is the problem; the person is not the problem.
- Problems can blind people from noticing and appreciating their strengths and capacity to find solutions. People have good intentions.
- People are doing the best they can.
- The power of change is within us.

Strengths-Based Practice with Children[6]

- Focus on strengths rather than weaknesses.
- Build authentic relationships with children and families.
- Facilitate children's services to others and their communities.
- Respect children's and families' right to self-determination.
- Believe that change is inevitable.
- Believe that all people and all communities have resources.
- Embrace empowerment as a process and a goal.
- Collaborate with children, families, and other professionals in the reclaiming process.

Spotlight 2. Principles of Solution-Focused Practice8

- *Resistance is not a useful concept.* When we describe young people as resistant, we imply they do not want to change. It indicates we operate from a position of power and that we know what is right.
- *Cooperation is inevitable.* When we practice from this stance, we let the young person lead, and we follow. From this perspective, we cooperate.
- *Change is inevitable.* Change is the only permanent thing in the universe; the only question is when it will begin.
- *Only a small change is needed.* When small changes are encouraged and noted, they lead to more change.
- *Most people already possess the resources they need to change.* There are already times when a young person does not show the problem in question. We help by exploring those times, so the person can do more of what works.
- *Problems are unsuccessful attempts to resolve conflicts.* People cope with challenges as they best can; at times, their coping is unsuccessful.
- *You do not need to know much about a problem to solve it.* It is more helpful and hopeful to explore what the person does differently or what is different at times when the problem is absent or lesser.
- *Clients define the goal of treatment.* When young people define the goal they want to accomplish, they are more likely to accomplish it.
- *Reality is observer-defined, and the therapist participates in co-creating the therapy system's reality.* All people filter their perceptions of reality to fit their experiences. We can help young people change the viewing of a situation.
- *There are many ways of looking at a situation, none more correct than others.* We must always be willing to look at a situation from different perspectives.

Positive psychology is the scientific study of the strengths that enable individuals and communities to thrive.[9] The field of positive psychology emerged in the United States in the late 1990s "to begin to catalyze a change in the focus of psychology from a preoccupation only with repairing the worst things in life to also building positive qualities."[10] Using his platform as the chair of the American Psychological Association, Martin Seligman called for both psychological research and practice to focus on what makes life most worth living. The study and application of positive psychology is now pursued around the world by researchers and practitioners in areas of health, well-being, psychotherapy, education, and character strengths. Positive psychology takes a balanced approach to people by exploring both their strengths and their challenges. It is equally concerned with healing the wounded and helping healthy people live fulfilled lives.

Spotlight 3. Positive Psychology

- Positive psychology studies what makes life most worth living.[11]
- Positive psychology is the scientific study of positive human functioning and flourishing on multiple levels including the biological, personal, relational, institutional, cultural, and global dimensions of life.[12]
- Positive psychology is the study of the conditions and processes that contribute to the flourishing or optimal functioning of people, groups, and institutions.[13]
- Positive psychology is the scientific study of human flourishing and an applied approach to optimal functioning. It also has been defined as the study of the strengths and virtues that enable individuals, communities, and organizations to thrive.[14]
- Positive psychology means different things to different people, depending on their theoretical perspectives and cultural backgrounds. There is, however, a unifying, underlying theme: Life can be made better for all people if certain conditions are met. Another characteristic of positive psychology is that it is dynamic, evolving, and ever expanding.[15]

Positive psychologists assert that people around the world, regardless of culture, religion, and history, share the hope of living a good life. Seligman identified five core elements necessary to the development of psychological well-being and happiness: positive emotion, engagement, relationships, meaning, and accomplishments.[16]

Positive Outcomes for All Young People

The purpose of this book is to give youth practitioners knowledge about psychosocial growth and development and provide intentional responsive adult practices to meet the developmental needs of young people. Figure 2 extends a model developed by the Center on the Developing Child at Harvard University and illustrates the impact of supportive and adverse experiences and environments on children's lives.[17] At one end of the scale are adverse childhood experiences and adverse community environments, underdeveloped strengths, and executive functions, along with a lack of supportive developmental relationships and support for the young person's culture and faith. For many children, this leads to intolerable toxic stress and negative outcomes. At the other end, leading to manageable stress and positive outcomes, are supportive families and environments that nurture strengths and executive functions, along with supportive developmental relationships and support for the young person's culture and faith. When children's growth needs are met, the scale tips toward positive outcomes. Young people can move from mere survival toward thriving. Supportive environments and caring adults can balance a child's scale and turn toxic stress into tolerable stress. Adding more resources (weight) to the positive side of the scale tips it toward positive outcomes for the young person.

In part III of this book, I describe ten intentional responsive adult practices. They are designed to increase the capacity of youth practitioners to support children and youth in achieving positive outcomes, daily and over time.

When young people are swamped by stress, and they lack the presence of adults, stress turns toxic and disrupts normal brain development, contributing to serious mental illness, problematic relationships, and learning difficulties. Mental and physical illnesses cost young people, families, and communities pain and hardship on many fronts and inevitably require specialized interventions and resources. The more support and weight youth practitioners can muster on the right side of the scale, the easier it is to turn the young person's trajectory toward positive outcomes.

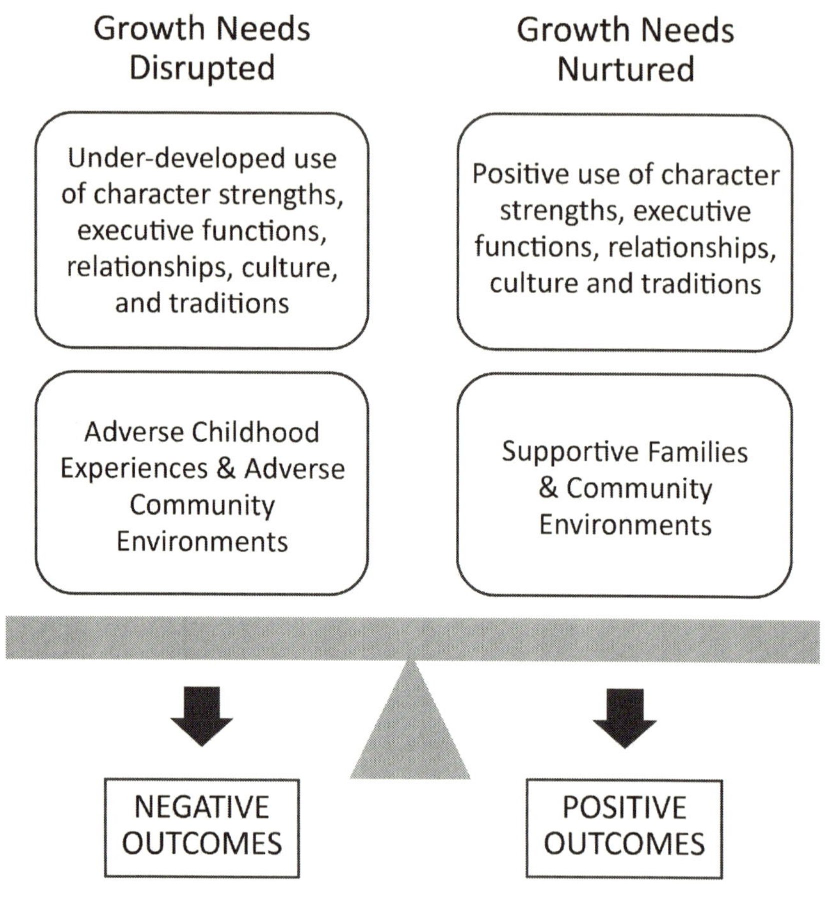

Figure 2. Impact of adverse and supportive experiences and environments

Outcomes, whether positive or negative, are expressed in thoughts, emotions, and behaviors. I recommend you turn to appendices A and B to explore the impact of positive and negative outcomes on child growth and development in more depth. Since young people function in concert with others, positive and negative experiences impact others across their ecology, fueling either pain or strengths. Youth practitioners who work with children and youth whose experiences have led them toward negative outcomes must learn to look behind the outward behaviors. They should strive to understand what happened to children and what goes on inside them—referred to as the "inside kid," a term coined by my friend Mark Freado.[19]

Reflections

- Reflect on the philosophy I have described. How does your personal philosophy fit with my philosophy?
- Identify three ways you can begin to focus on strengths rather than weaknesses.

Explorations

- Listen to Martin Seligman's TED Talk, "The New Era of Positive Psychology."[18]
- Listen to Christopher Peterson's talks, "What Makes Life Worth Living?"[19]
- Read the article by Martin Seligman et al., "Positive education: Positive psychology and classroom interventions."[20]
- Read Christopher Peterson's book *A Primer in Positive Psychology.*[21]
- Listen to Ricardo Arguís Rey's TED Talk, "The Future of Happiness."[22]
- Read Ricardo Arguís Rey et al.'s book, *The "Happy Classrooms" Programme: Positive psychology applied to education.*[23]

2

Pathways to Thriving

I have asked hundreds of parents what they want for their children when they grow up. I jotted down their answers, and about four years ago I pulled out the notes and searched them for common themes. I was not surprised to find a common theme - parents want their children to be happy and have a good life. Their hopes for their children are expressed in the following:

A good life means

living in a place where you feel connected and relatedness,

being with people you love,

becoming the best you can,

doing the right things—with hope and purpose,

and contributing to the community.

Parents and other caring adults want all young people to develop and thrive and to be on a growth pathway, despite challenges, adversity, and traumatic experiences. Young people also strive to grow emotionally, socially, intellectually, spiritually, and physically. Growth is not a destination but a process to become stronger. *Merriam-Webster* defines growth as "the process of growing; progressive development; evolution; increase or expansion"—the continued strengthening of social, emotional, social, physical, and spiritual development.

Developmental psychologists and scientists in the fields of child development, positive psychology, resilience, and positive youth development have identified universal human needs essential to positive outcomes and well-being. The different fields converge and identify psychosocial needs that are essential for healthy growth and development. Meeting these needs motivates people to pursue well-being, strengthen their buffers against adversity, and develop resilience. I refer to five growths needs as follows:

- Belonging in an ecology of relatedness
- Achievement of goals and coping with challenges
- Autonomy to regulate emotions and actions
- Contributing to others and the community
- Hope and purpose

Abraham Maslow referred to a hierarchy of needs, including safety, belonging, self-esteem, self-actualization, and (later) transcendence.[24] The National Center on the Developing Child at Harvard University[25] identified protective factors that promote resilience. These factors are responsive relationships with supportive and caring adults, flexible coping skills and self-regulation, self-efficacy and perceived control, and contexts that support cultural traditions or faith. Martin Seligman, the father of positive psychology, theorized that well-being is achieved through positive emotions, engagement, relationships, meaning, and achievement/accomplishments.[26] Karen Pittman identified connection, competence, character, confidence, and contribution (the 5 Cs) as essential pathways to achieve positive youth development outcomes.[27] Richard Lerner added caring as an additional goal to develop productive and well-functioning adults.[28] In Response Ability Pathways, Larry Brendtro and Lesley du Toit used the four needs identified by the Circle of Courage: belonging, mastery, independence, and generosity.[29]

Table 1. Universal growth needs—pathways to resilience and thriving

Growth Needs Laursen, 2018	Hierarchy of Needs Maslow, 2013 Koltko-Rivera, 2006	Protective Factors The National Scientific Council on the Developing Child, 2015	Elements of Well-being Seligman, 2011	Positive Youth Development Pittman, 2003 Lerner, 2007	Circle of Courage Brendtro, Brokenleg, & van Bockern, 2002
Belonging	Belonging	Responsive Relationships	Relationships	Connection	Belonging
Achievement	Self-esteem	Adaptive coping	Accomplishments	Competence	Mastery
Autonomy	Self-actualization	Self-efficacy and self-regulation	Positive emotion	Character/ Confidence	Independence
Contributing	Transcendence	Cultural traditions and faith	Engagement	Contribution/ Caring	Generosity
Hope and Purpose			Meaning		

People, young and old, are motivated to meet these growth needs because their brains are hard-wired to do so. When young people have the strengths, capacities, and supports to overcome challenges and face adversity, connections in the brain become stronger and contribute to positive outcomes. On the other hand, an inability to learn from failure, problems, and challenges causes emotional and social distress that disrupts biosocial growth and brain development, leading to negative outcomes.

When young people meet the needs for belonging, achievement, autonomy, contribution, and hope and purpose, they thrive and experience well-being and happiness. Young people who are unable to meet these needs struggle with learning and relationships, have little hope, and are left with a poor sense of purpose. Children and youth who grow up with chronic, unpredictable, and unresolved stress often lack the necessary support to meet their needs. The result for many are painful emotions, painful thoughts, and pain-based behaviors. When caring adults team up with young people to turn toxic stress into tolerable stress, they can help young people effectively harness their desire for positive experiences and outcomes.

Belonging in an Ecology of Relatedness

> The Earth does not belong to man; Man belongs to the Earth. This we know. All things are connected, like the blood which unites one family. We do not weave the web of life. Whatever befalls the Earth befalls the sons of the Earth. Man did not weave the web of life, he is merely a strand in it. Whatever he does to the web, he does to himself.
>
> —Chief Seattle

Belonging in an ecology of relatedness is a universal growth need.[30] It makes people feel valued, important, and protected by others. When people experience belonging, they feel comfortable and welcome—in a family, with friends, and in the community. Young people who are strongly connected to people, community, and the ecology feel significant. Connectedness is experienced and is not a cognitive process; rather, it describes a healthy, protective relationship between youth and the environments in which they grow up.[31] Connectedness, or belongingness, differs from instantaneous and short-term connections with individual adults. It implies a sense of place, respect, and belonging that comes from their feeling included, knowing that others like them and experiencing that they are valued members of the community.

The family and close community are the most important influences on belonging.[32] Those who have a weak sense of belonging due to a disrupted or unsupportive upbringing can rebuild or strengthen their sense of belonging by developing close allegiances, friendships, and relationships later in life. With broken belongingness, people may have difficulty relating to others. They may join or identify with negative groups that promote crime, religious hatred, homophobia, or other distorted views.

Connections with negative influences are attempts to feel important and accepted within a social structure. Young people with disrupted relations may become nonresponsive or resistant to the efforts of positive people and groups, including counselors and teachers, because they do not feel worthy of inclusion, or they fear being rejected by positive people in the future. They scare off those with whom they most want to be connected.

Resilience researchers have identified that the caring relationship with a positive adult is the strongest protective factor a young person can have.[33] At least one caring adult is essential to the young person's brain to develop secure attachment and to regulate affect arousal. In the absence of caring adults, the brain's circuitry develops loose connections, resulting in poor coping skills.

Achievement of Goals and Coping with Challenges

> Personal mastery is not something you possess. It is a process. People with a high level of personal mastery are acutely aware of their ignorance, their incompetence, their growth areas. And they are deeply self-confident. Paradoxical? Only for those who do not see the "journey is the reward."
>
> —Peter Senge[34]

Mastery, or achievement, is the desire to get better at things that matter. People want to learn and improve, whether it is cooking, swimming, speaking a foreign language, fixing a car, playing an instrument, making friends, overcoming adversity, or finding purpose in their lives. People have an innate desire to learn and to master the world around them. Achievement is an essential building block of human growth.[35] It propels people to develop and use knowledge, skills, and abilities and to develop a value system that can anchor them. And it provides experiences of success and competence. Achievement is the foundation of self-esteem and motivates people to make the next leap toward mastery. Supportive adults and environments provide a multitude of experiences for a child to build a strong sense of mastery and success as a learner.

Young people with a strong sense of achievement feel competent in their abilities and seek more challenges and knowledge. They are willing to fail and to look unskilled when they try new things. As a result, they develop perseverance and a passion for long-term goals, and they are more likely to be successful and curious. The pathways to achievement can be demanding and exhilarating because of unexpected challenges and adversities.

With an impaired sense of mastery, young people may develop a low self-concept, refuse to try new things for fear of failure, give up easily, become dependent on others, or devalue and ridicule schooling or the efforts of others. Some young people mask their lack of achievement with rebellious and reckless behaviors. They may take excessive risks; become manipulative, arrogant, or delinquent; and engage in early sexual activities.

Autonomy to Regulate Emotions and Actions

> The greatest gift you can give your children are the roots of responsibility and the wings of independence.
>
> —Denis Waitley

People are born to exert their will to develop a sense of autonomy.[36] Early in life, children show this by wanting to feed themselves or walk without the support of a caregiver. Developing a sense of control and responsibility for one's thinking, emotions, and actions is a core psychological growth need. Later in life, the drive for autonomy and responsibility contributes to self-reliance, self-efficacy, and self-determination.

The human brain is capable of developing language, introspection, abstract reasoning, problem solving, and decision making. Young people pursue autonomy by asserting their voices about issues that are important to them and by increasingly associating with their peers. They are engaged in an intriguing dance, balancing their need for individuality and being in community with others.[37] At times, young people focus more on themselves, and at other times, they focus more on being communal.

People with a strong sense of independence and responsibility are in control of themselves. They understand that autonomy does not mean doing everything alone or just to meet their own needs. They know that being in community with others includes collaboration, shared responsibility, and, at times, compromises. Young people with a lessened or absent sense of independence are likely to engage in "scatterbrained" behavior and to be easily swayed by others. Rather than taking responsibility for their emotions and actions, they often project blame on events and other people.

Contributing to Others and the Community

> Everybody can be great. Because everybody can serve. You don't have to have a college degree to serve. You don't have to make your subject and verb agree to serve. You don't have to know about Plato and Aristotle to serve. You don't have to know Einstein's Theory of Relativity to serve. You don't have to know the Second Theory of Thermal Dynamics in Physics to serve. You only need a heart full of grace. A soul generated by love.[38]
>
> —Martin Luther King Jr.

From an early age, children naturally help others in need. When acknowledged and appreciated for helping, they beam with pride. Benevolence and making a difference to others is a universal need for humans.[39] Without it, the human species would not survive.

People are programmed to prefer helping over hurting, as illustrated by these examples:

- When nine-month-old children can choose whether to play with climbing toys, helper toys, or hurter toys, they rarely pick the last.[40]
- When eighteen-month-old children see an adult drop a clothespin without any affect, they don't do anything, but when the adult shows emotional distress, the kids will pick it up and give it to the adult.[41]

Later in life, when we see a baby who needs food or comfort or a person who is suffering, hurting, and needing help, we instinctually reach out and give—time, money, food, or clothes. We are programmed to make a difference to others, but this predisposition to make a difference to others must be nurtured. Adults must provide opportunities for kids to develop this sense of responsibility, compassion, and social conscience.[42]

People with a strong sense of compassion and empathy for others experience the joy of giving and receive pleasure from helping. People with a lower or absent sense of benevolence tend to be stingy and lack concern for the welfare of others, tend to be callous in their interactions, and take, rather than give. Many young people with abuse histories believe they can count only on themselves. They are often self-centered and place their own needs before anything or anyone else. Nevertheless, when given opportunities to help others, they are ready to put their own needs aside and go to work. Youth practitioners can support young people in meeting the need contributing by engaging them in service-learning activities in the community.

Hope and Purpose

> One cannot lead a life that is truly excellent without feeling that one belongs to something greater and more permanent than oneself.[43]
>
> —Mihaly Csikszentmihalyi

> Hope is the belief that the future will be better than the present, along with the belief that you have the power to make it so.[44]
>
> —Shane Lopez

People yearn to find meaning and purpose in their lives because it affirms their self-worth, their place in history, and their spiritual well-being.[45] People with a purpose are happier and healthier and live longer, and it is the reason they get up in the morning.[46] There are multiple pathways to discovering one's purpose (e.g., caring for others, the environment, or animals; developing free software; engaging in a social justice cause at the local, national, or global level).

Without hope, people are unlikely to have purpose. Research shows that 89 percent of people worldwide are hopeful about the future. Young people who grow up with chronic, unpredictable stress often feel hopeless. In the United States, just over half of young people feel hopeful about the future and feel they have some influence over it.[47] Finding ways to help young people experience hope and purpose is essential to well-being and achieving positive outcomes. "Hope is worth a letter grade in school and in one day's work," said psychologist Shane Lopez.[48] In controlled studies, he found that hopeful students can attribute one letter grade to their hope, and that hopeful people are 20 percent more productive than people without hope. Brain scans show that people in a complete resting state, by default, think about the future. In other words, they daydream and imagine possibilities. Amazingly, these future dreams create memories in the brain. When given the opportunity to tell stories about the future, people can bring up these memories and edit them. By doing so, they are on their way to creating their future.

When living with high levels of stress, many young people rarely, if ever, achieve a true resting state where they can daydream. When the entire brain bandwidth is committed to scanning and preparing for danger, they have no brain resources left to daydreaming. Youth practitioners can use this awareness to create safe places where young people can daydream and be engaged in talking about their hopes for the future.

Summary

The five growth needs fall along a continuum. At one end, the focus is on "I"; at the other, the focus is on "we." Andras Angyal, an American psychiatrist, and Urie Bronfenbrenner, a developmental psychologist, asserted than human development is deeply connected to the ecology in which a person grows up.[49] The I/we dimension of human growth is a dance and balancing act between meeting personal needs and community needs. The needs for achievement, autonomy, and hope and purpose fall on the "I" side of the continuum, while the needs for belonging and contribution fall on the "we" side of the continuum.

Reflections

- What do you want for children (including your own) when they are twenty-five years old?
- Does your practice reflect your hope for children?
- How do the five growth needs relate to the needs you support in young people?
- Think of a way you can support a young person to achieve each growth need.

Explorations

- Read *Supportive relationships and active skill-building strengthen the foundations of resilience: Working Paper 13.*[50]
- Read *Deep Brain Learning: Evidence-based essentials in education, treatment, and youth development* by Larry K. Brendtro and Martin L. Mitchell.[51]

3

Typical Brain Development

> Without understanding the basic principles of how the brain develops, we cannot expect to design and implement effective interventions.[52]
>
> —Bruce Perry and Erin Hambrick

Though this is not a book on neuroscience, knowledge of the brain helps youth practitioners understand how experiences influence brain development. With this awareness, they can learn to respond to children and youth in a supportive and brain-informed way. Learning about the brain's role in disruptive and impulsive behavior equips adults to look beyond behavior and ask, "What happened to this young person?" When youth practitioners find the answers to that question, they can respond to the immediate need of a young person in crisis, rather than reacting and attempting to control the situation.

Brain Essentials

The brain sits on top of the brain stem. It is approximately the size of two fists and weighs about three pounds. Different models of the brain depict this very complex system. The triune brain model, developed by Paul MacLean[53], provides a good understanding of the main principles of brain development and functionality. The triune model illustrates three major processing regions of the brain.

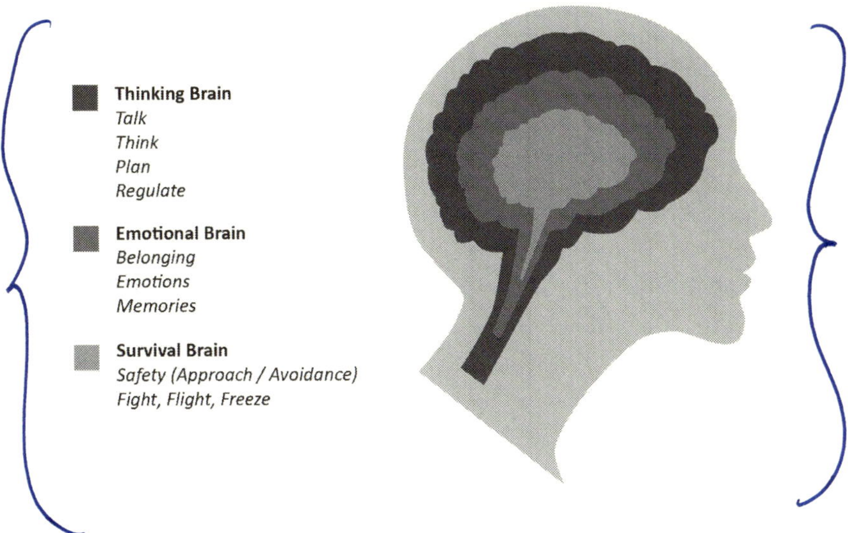

Figure 3. The triune brain

The survival brain, also called the reptilian brain, controls vital body functions such as heartbeat, blood pressure, breathing, body temperature, digestion, and balance. It includes the cerebellum and connects the brain to the brainstem. It is always turned on and always reacts; it never thinks. It can increase heart rate and blood circulation when it detects nearby danger and can slow the same down when there is no danger.

The emotional brain, also called the limbic brain, is responsible for our emotions. It links emotions and cognition and is the center for value judgment. Memories and experiences, positive as well as negative, are recorded in the limbic brain and help people know what to fear and what to approach. The main structures in the emotional brain are the amygdala, hippocampus, and hypothalamus.

The amygdala—or more correctly, the amygdalae, because we have two of them—is an almond-shaped structure that serves as the brain's security system. It detects threat and safety. It reacts to physical, emotional, social, or cultural threats within a second and can bypass the other structures in the limbic brain. In dangerous or threatening situations, it sends messages directly to the reptilian brain, releasing a stress hormone called cortisol.

When this happens, other brain functions, such as problem solving and learning, stop. This is called an amygdala hijack and results in a fight-flight-or-freeze response.

The hippocampus serves as the depository for our memories, both short-term and long-term memories. It is the center of our working memory, where we connect new impressions with previous memories to make meaning of concepts, skills, facts, etc.[54]

All sensory information that comes to the brain (except smell) passes through the thalamus and is then sent to other parts of the brain to be processed.

The thinking brain, or the cortex, is the center for language, abstract thinking, consciousness, imagination, and self-regulation. The cortex is divided into regions called lobes—the frontal, parietal, occipital, and temporal lobes—which perform different functions. The foremost part of the cortex, the prefrontal cortex, is of great interest because it is the command center for executive functioning skills, such as self-regulation, planning, and organization.

Cells That Fire Together, Wire Together

The average adult brain has about one hundred billion cells, called neurons. Each cell may connect to tens of thousands of other brain cells through their synapses, which are the junctions between two neurons. The neurons connect to one another to control body, behavior, thought, and emotion.

Every experience, thought, feeling, and physical sensation triggers thousands of neurons. Repetition of the same experiences triggers the same neurons each time to form a neural network. This process is referred to as "cells that fire together, wire together". Wiring means that neurons that are repeatedly activated develop pathways wrapped in an insulating layer of fatty substance called myelin, which protects the neuron and helps it conduct signals more efficiently.

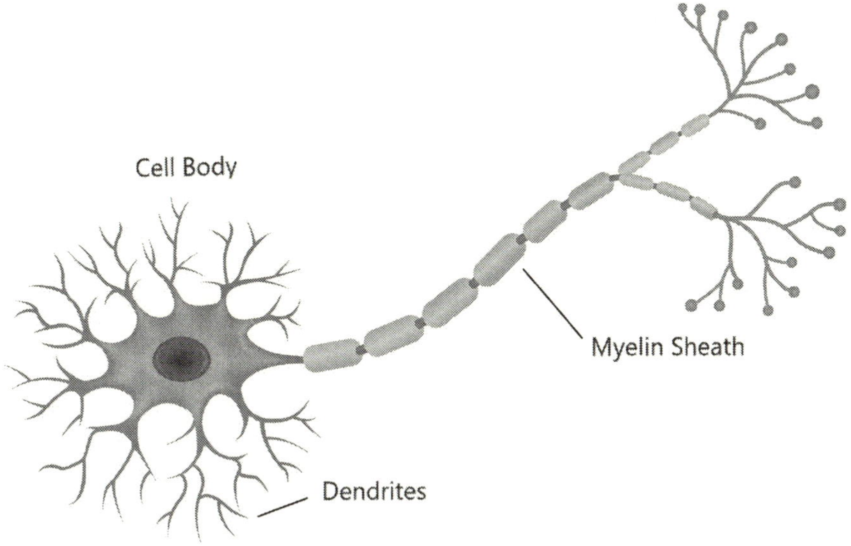

Figure 4. The neuron

Use It or Lose It

From infancy through the onset of puberty, synaptic connections are pruned, like trimming weak branches from a bush, so the rest can grow stronger. This is known as "use it or lose it." During certain periods of life, the brain is more active in removing unnecessary neural connections. Some pruning takes place very early in life, though the most rapid pruning happens around age three and age sixteen. Different parts of the brain go through pruning during different periods. Pruning, also called apoptosis, is an essential part of brain development because it gets rid of connections that are less used and gives room for important connections, making the brain more efficient. The pruning process is influenced by the environment and affects learning. For example, languages are easily learned before age twelve. After that, unused connections are pruned, making new languages harder to learn.

The Brain Develops Bottom Up and Back to Front

The brain begins forming about three weeks after conception and continues to develop throughout life, though some periods of life are characterized by more profound development than others. The survival brain begins to develop soon after conception, followed by the midbrain and the cortex. Neural connectivity begins in the back of the brain and then slowly matures from the bottom up and from the back to the front. The very last parts to connect are the frontal lobes, the seat of self-regulation, emotional control, and other executive functions. The prefrontal cortex is the last to mature in the mid-twenties.[55]

Figure 5 shows the results of magnetic resonance imaging, or MRI. It illustrates the increase of myelination with age, from the bottom up and back to the front. Unconnected areas (lighter) are called gray matter and contain numerous cell bodies and dendrites and relatively few myelinated axons. Myelinated pathways (darker)—connected networks—are called white matter because the fatty substance used for myelination is white.

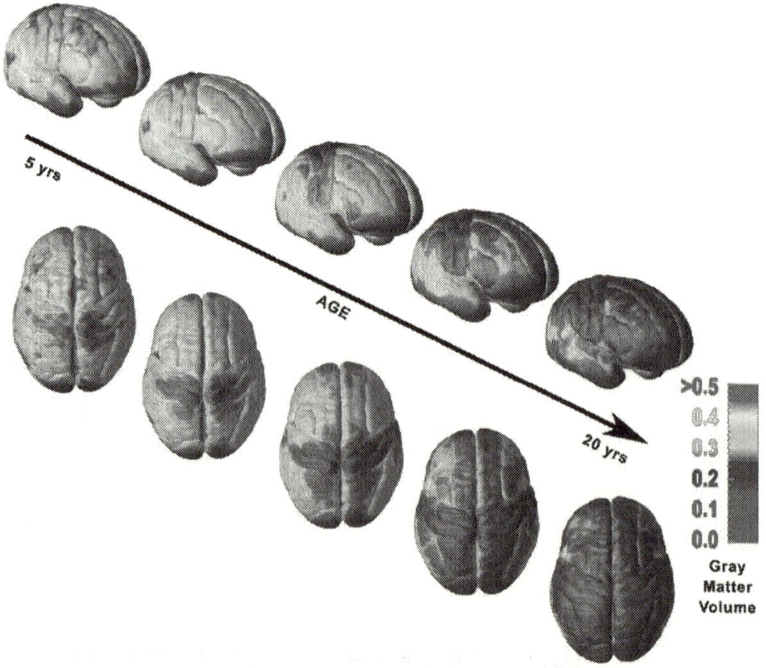

Figure 5. Gray matter volume decreases with age

Brain Plasticity

The development of abilities such as vision, walking, and speech are called *experience expectant* because most children who grow up in "good enough" situations develop these abilities. For example, almost all environments are saturated with language, and children learn to communicate with words without special stimulation. Similarly, children do not need special experiences to develop vision. Brain systems that regulate more complex abilities, on the other hand, are *experience dependent.* From infancy, such systems are strengthened through the process known as *serve and return.*[56] Serve and return works like a game of tennis—the infant serves with gestures, babbling, touch, eye contact, or facial expressions. A responsive adult returns the serve with laughing, playing peek-a-boo, speaking, or caressing the child. Through serve-and-return experiences, children learn to regulate their emotions during stress and build the foundation for strong self-regulation later in life.

Brain systems that regulate complex abilities are more malleable to experience.[57] In other words, they are dependent on children's experiences as they grow up. Planning, regulating emotions, and relationships are examples of more complex abilities. These experience-dependent abilities are also called executive functions.

Let us look at the development of two domains of executive functioning: inhibition and shifting.[58] Inhibition is the ability to resist impulses and to stop behavior at the appropriate time. It emerges during the first seven to eight months, and by the age of four, a child has developed the ability to inhibit impulses related to simple tasks and shows signs of regulating impulses to more complex tasks. Under healthy conditions, inhibition continues to improve from age five to eight, particularly for tasks that combine inhibition with working memory, the ability to hold necessary information available for processing. Mastery of inhibition is typically developed by age twelve.

Preschoolers begin to develop the ability to shift and transition between simple tasks, tolerate change, and engage in flexible problem solving.

The ability to shift between more complex tasks develops in conjunction with the development of working memory between the ages of seven and nine. By mid-adolescence, they have typically reached adult-like levels. While children are wired with the potential to develop these and other domains of executive functions, the development of executive functions are experience-dependent, meaning they require the support and modeling of caring adults.

During the first three years of life, the brain is extremely dependent on experiences while its basic architecture is being built.[59] Genes provide the road map, and experiences determine which genes are turned on or off. Based on the child's experiences, a solid or unstable framework is laid down that determines future learning, behavior, and health.

Much attention has been directed at understanding the importance of a child's experiences during the first three years of life, and one might think that the chances to influence brain connections during middle age and adolescence are few. The teenage years, however, are a critical time, when the brain, again, is particularly sensitive to experiences.[60] While adolescents may look like adults, their brain systems have only about 80 percent of the capacity of an adult in areas such as relationships, impulse regulation, focusing, planning, and following through.[61] During adolescence, the least integrated parts of the brain—the frontal and prefrontal cortex—undergo major integration with brain regions that regulate the experience of pleasure, the way we view and think about other people, and our ability to exercise self-control. This involves the reward system, the relationship system, and the regulatory system—the three R's of adolescent brain development.[62]

Neuroscientists note that the brain does not require exceptional conditions for normal development. Good-enough support from caring adults and supportive environments are sufficient to establish healthy connections and create pathways to well-being and happiness.

Reflections

- How can/does neuroscience influence your work with young people?
- How do you currently respond to kids who act impulsively or violently or who withdraw?
- Identify steps you can take to respond rather than react in such situations.

Explorations

- Read *How the Brain Learns* by David Sousa.[63]
- Read *Age of Opportunity: Lessons from the Science of Adolescence* by Lawrence Steinberg.[64]

PART II

Child and Adolescent Growth Disrupted

4

Psycho-Social Pain

A Story of Pain and Resilience

> I started having nightmares ... In them, our family was united and then divided over and over again. Always, we were on the brink of separation in my dreams, the difference hinging on a decision of mine. Always, at the last minute before waking up, I made the wrong call that divided us one more time. The pain was fresh each time it happened.[65]
>
> —Liz Murray

Liz Murray's autobiography, *Breaking Night*, describes her tumultuous life growing up.[66] She was born to loving and drug-addicted parents. During her first three years of life, while her father served a prison term for selling prescription drugs, her mother was relatively drug-free and attended to the needs of Liz and her sister, Lisa. Shortly after her father returned from prison, both parents resumed their drug use, which escalated over the following years. Liz and Lisa fended for themselves as they best could, watching their parents mainline cocaine in plain view, experiencing emotional and physical neglect, and being exposed to chronic, unpredictable, and unresolved stress. Her mother's schizophrenia, alcoholism, and legal blindness added to the chaos—the apartment was untidy, and she didn't attend to her children's clothes. Regularly, the family's monthly welfare check was spent on drugs rather than food, leaving Liz scavenging for food in trashcans.

As their drug use intensified, her parents grew apart. Liz's mother ventured into the community more and more often to hook up with other drug users and people who could support her drug use. During a visit with her mother at the home of one of these connections, Liz was sexually molested. Liz told her mother what had happened, and the mother stopped the relationship immediately. Liz blamed herself, however, for causing one of her mom's breakdowns, which resulted in hospitalization. As a child, Liz did not understand that her mom's breakdown was triggered by her schizophrenia and the fact that she had acquired AIDS.

Until Liz began school, she had no idea how different her family was from other families. She believed that her parents attended to her and Lisa's needs, "or whatever they didn't tend to didn't matter because I had no clue that I needed anything more … Things were sometimes tough, but we had each other and having that, we had it all."[67] In school, she was teased because of her odor, her torn and dirty clothes, and her lice-infested hair. Realizing that her family was not normal, she never felt any belonging in school. She escaped the pain of not belonging by skipping school. Eventually, at age thirteen, the child welfare system caught up with her truancy and took custody of her. She was placed in a girl's residential home for a few months. Until then, she had squeezed by in school and was passed on from year to year by showing up to take—and pass—the standardized tests. Her father's extensive knowledge and numerous unreturned library books had been her main resource for any academic learning she accomplished. Liz's life circumstances allowed her to pursue the growth needs of achievement and autonomy, while she had fewer opportunities to meet her needs for belonging, contribution, and hope and purpose.

During the time Liz was at the girl's residential center, her mom and Lisa moved in with the mother's boyfriend. Upon her discharge from the residential center, Liz lived at the boyfriend's home with her mom and Lisa for a short while. Finding it overwhelming to be part of her mother's deteriorating health, Liz left, and at age fifteen, she was homeless. She carried everything she owned in her backpack and slept at friends' houses after their parents had gone to work, under bridges, and in stairwells of random apartment buildings, or she rode the subway all night to stay warm. She rarely had access to a shower and scavenged for anything to eat. When she couldn't find any food, she stole wherever and whenever she could.

During this time, Liz hooked up with a young man who had grown up on the streets, hustling and running drugs. Shortly after she met him, he grew increasingly violent. One evening, at a cheap motel, he became angry and punched his hand into the wall next to her face before he stormed out. After he left, Liz heard on the TV that a woman had just been murdered by her boyfriend a few rooms away in the same motel. She realized it could just as well have been her. A few months later, her mother died from AIDS. These two events catalyzed Liz to apply to an alternative high school a friend had told her about.

With the help of supportive teachers and staff, she set the goal to graduate from high school in two years with a straight-A average—and did so. One of the teachers encouraged her to apply for the *New York Times* college scholarship, which she won. Liz applied to Brown and Harvard and enrolled at Harvard in the fall of 2000.[68] She struggled both academically and socially during the first semester and did not return for the second semester. By this time, her winning essay to the *New York Times* had given her speaking engagements, book offers, and talks about a film. She was also drawn to her friends and family in New York and explained that "it's just not a good time for me to be in college."[69] Over the next years, she coproduced the film about her life, spoke and wrote about her experiences growing up, and supported her ailing father until he died from AIDS in 2006.[70]

When you have read the chapter about adverse childhood experiences and adverse community environments, reflect on how many of these may have been Liz's experiences growing up.

Pain and More Pain

Liz Murray worried about the pain she caused her mom by telling her about being sexually abused, and she felt guilty that she caused her mother to be hospitalized. Liz was haunted by nightmares that she had caused the breakup of her family by skipping school. Liz was flooded by pain that controlled many of her emotions, thoughts, and behaviors. *Pain-based emotions* include feelings of loneliness, failure, sadness, shame, fear, and anger.[71] Painful emotions have multiple names, but they all have in common that they typically receive less empathy from others than physical pain, and they are triggered by memories, while physical pain is not. Unresolved painful emotions are likely to negatively influence self-esteem and mental health in the long term. *Pain-based thoughts* include guilt, distrust, hatred, helplessness, and unworthiness.[72] To cope with intrusive painful thoughts and feelings, people often use defense mechanisms—coping strategies—such as blaming others or themselves, rationalizing, repression, minimizing, and denial. *Pain-based behaviors* are triggered by deep-seated psychoemotional pain and are expressed along a continuum that stretches from acting out to acting in.[73] The outside and visible behaviors on this continuum include impulsive outbursts, aggression, risky behaviors (drugs, sex), running away, inability to tolerate uncertainty and ambiguity, anxiety, withdrawal, self-harm, traumatic reenactment, and flashbacks. Liz did not take her pain out on others. Rather, she turned her pain inwards by

- escaping the pain by skipping school;
- internalizing the pain by blaming herself for her mother's hospitalization;
- repressing the pain by leaving to be on her own and becoming homeless; and
- agonizing about the pain that she caused the breakup of the family and blaming herself.

Other survivors of abuse and neglect also describe the pain they felt from the chronic and unpredictable stress experienced at the hands of the people on whom they depended the most.[74] Brian Raychaba, who himself grew up in a violent home, interviewed Canadian youth who had been removed from their families to live in foster care settings.[75] The young people shared their feelings of powerlessness and the pain of being separated from their families because of events over which they had no control. Under their pain, they hungered for caring relationships and a sense of control and involvement in decisions about their lives. Though the pain was obvious to the young people themselves, the youth practitioners who were charged with helping them rarely understood their pain.

James Anglin interviewed youth and staff in residential programs in Canada about their experiences.[76] He also found a pattern of pain and reported that the chronic and acute pain experienced by young people is expressed in two forms: physical pain and psychoemotional pain. The young people shared that psychoemotional pain often overshadow physical pain. though it is less recognized and understood by youth practitioners. Anglin called the behavioral responses to deeply felt pain *pain-based behaviors.*

Anglin found that youth workers often are unaware of young people's pain, and they also are ill-prepared and unable to respond therapeutically in unpredictable and volatile situations. In addition, many youth workers have their own unresolved pain triggered during such interactions, resulting in their own pain-based behaviors. Thus, many adults who are expected to support children but who have experienced chronic and unpredictable stress themselves react to their own frustrations, rather than responding to the pain and the needs of the young people.[16]

From Pain to Resilience

Let's return to Liz Murray's story. She graduated from Harvard University in 2006 and was awarded an honorary doctorate degree of public service from Merrimack University in 2013.[77] Today, she is an inspirational speaker and works with homeless youth in a shelter in New York, helping them discover their strengths and articulate their hopes for their future.[78]

Regardless of both parents' drug use and her mother also being an alcoholic, legally blind, and struggling with schizophrenia, Liz always knew she was loved. "Forgiveness came very naturally to me. People can't give you what they don't have. My parents were mentally ill and drug addicted. I understood they were not really malicious toward me. They loved me, and I loved them," said Liz Murray in an interview.[79]

Her father was an avid reader, a lexicon of knowledge, and Liz attributes her interest in learning and reading to him. As a child, she joined him in scavenging expeditions in the community and learned important lessons that were imprinted into her life: other people's throwaways may be your treasure; be who you are; and don't let other people tell you what you should be like. Her father also showed her how to find odd jobs to make money. Liz developed a keen awareness of the need to connect with other people, often to satisfy her hunger. She developed friendships with others and was often invited to join them at mealtimes.

During her mother's last days of life, Liz promised to turn her own life around. "Like my mother, I was always saying, 'I'll fix my life one day.' It became clear when I saw her die without fulfilling her dreams that my time was now or maybe never."[80]

Liz Murray's story is also a story of resilience. It highlights the importance of the being loved and the power of genetics. Liz Murray's internal resources and external supports were instrumental to the paths she took during her childhood and adolescent years. In chapter 8, I discuss how people can use their character strengths as leverage to overcome adversity. I have no doubt that Liz's resilience was fueled by her character strengths, but Liz could not have known the names of her character strengths, since the framework was first published in 2004.[81] Liz wrote that education saved her life, that she was always loved by her parents, that forgiveness came easy to her, and that she was determined to earn her high school diploma with straight A's. Comments like these—and many others throughout her autobiography and in interviews—suggest that that her signature strengths may include forgiveness, love of learning, love, perseverance, and bravery. Liz Murray had an incredible ability to use her strengths throughout her childhood and adolescent years.

Reflections

- Identify the pain-based behaviors in some of the young people with whom you work.
- How do you respond to kids who show pain-based behaviors?
- What is one thing you can do more of to respond to pain-based behaviors?

Explorations

- Read *The Boy Who Was Raised as a Dog* by Bruce Perry and Maia Szalavitz.[82]
- Read *Reaching and Teaching Children Who Hurt* by Susan A. Craig.[83]

5

Adverse Experiences in the Home and the Community

Adverse Childhood Experiences

Many children grow up in families filled with stress. Vincent Felitti, Robert Anda, and their colleagues collected data to study the connection between adverse childhood experiences (ACEs) in the family before age eighteen and lifelong health and wellness outcomes.[84] Between 1995 and 1997, seventeen thousand mostly white, college-educated people with jobs and good health insurance participated in the study.

The adverse childhood experiences study asked ten questions about childhood maltreatment and family dysfunction during the first eighteen years of the participants' lives.[85] Participants were instructed to check the number one if they had experienced the event and zero if not. Adding up the number of ones checked generated a person's ACE score.

Spotlight 4. Adverse Childhood Experiences

Household Dysfunction

- Addicted to alcohol or other substance
- Losing a parent to divorce, separation, or other reason
- Mental illness
- Witnessing mother being abused/battered
- A household member in prison

Abuse

- Verbal/psychological
- Physical
- Sexual

Neglect

- Emotional
- Physical

In addition to the confidential survey, information was collected about the participants' current health and behaviors. The information was combined with the results of a physical examination to form the baseline data for the study.

The major findings of the study noted that 64 percent of the participants had an ACE score of 1 or more, and 12 percent had an ACE score of 4 or more. The researchers found that the higher the ACE score, the greater the risk for chronic disease, mental illness, violence, or being a victim of violence. For example, a person with an ACE score of 4, compared to someone with an ACE score of 0, was twelve times more likely to attempt suicide, seven times more likely to become an alcoholic, and twice as likely to develop heart disease. Table 6 shows other health risks associated with a person's ACE score.

Table 2. ACE scores and high-risk behaviors

With 0 ACEs	With 3 ACEs	With 7+ ACEs
1 in 16 smokes	1 in 9 smokes	1 in 6 smokes
1 in 69 is alcoholic	1 in 17 is alcoholic	1 in 8 is alcoholic
1 in 480 uses IV drugs	1 in 43 uses IV drugs	1 in 30 uses IV drugs
1 in 14 has heart disease	1 in 7 has heart disease	1 in 6 has heart disease
1 in 96 attempts suicide	1 in 10 attempts suicide	1 in 5 attempts suicide
1 in 17 has intercourse by age 15	1 in 5 has intercourse by age 15	1 in 3 has intercourse by age 15

Adapted from Anda & Felitti[86]

According to Vincent Felitti, one of the ACE study's primary researchers, none of the ACEs trumps another in terms of seriousness or consequences. It appears, though, that extreme neglect—for example, as experienced by children in Romanian orphanages during Ceausescu's regime—is more damaging to brain development than other forms of maltreatment.[87] The ACE study questions are used as a framework to understand the stressors in children's lives across the world.

Adverse Community Environments

Stressful experiences outside the family also can result in extended activation of the stress response system and disrupt healthy development. Adverse community experiences may include poverty, discrimination, community violence, lack of opportunity, economic mobility, and social mobility.[88]

Data from the 2016 National Survey of Children's Health show that one-fourth of American children have experienced one ACE. Another 21.7 percent of children have had two or more ACEs. Children growing up in poverty are at the highest risk.[89] The survey found that 37 percent of children living at or below the poverty level had two or more adverse childhood experiences, as compared to 19 percent of children raised in families with incomes twice the poverty level, and 9 percent among children living in families with incomes higher than four times the federal poverty level. While one-third of children living at or below the poverty level had no adverse experiences, the likelihood of growing up with no ACEs decreases with higher family incomes. Children living with family incomes twice the poverty level increases the absence of experiencing an ACE to 43 percent and to 74 percent for children living at more than four times the poverty level.[90]

African American, Hispanic, and other, non-Hispanic children in the US are more likely to live in poverty than white children (36 percent, 32 percent, 20 percent, and 13 percent, respectively). Consequently, it is no surprise that children of color are at higher risk of ACEs than white children. African American children and youth are more likely than their white and Hispanic peers to have had two or more adverse experiences (34 percent, 19 percent, 22 percent, respectively). On the flipside, white children are most likely to grow up with no adverse experiences, followed by Hispanic and African American children (59 percent, 49 percent, 36 percent, respectively).[91]

Children in foster care are at disproportionately higher risk of ACEs, as compared to other children living with elevated risks, such as growing up in poverty, being of color, or being raised by single mothers. Children enter foster care because of abuse, neglect, and other adversities, such as parental substance abuse, parental mental health issues, and domestic violence. A recent study showed that children in foster care or adopted from foster care experienced parental divorce or separation, parental death, parental incarceration, parental abuse, exposure to violence, household member mental illness, and household member substance abuse at higher rates than their counterparts in the general population.[92]

While foster care currently may be the only option for some children, it should be short term and with a focus on family reunification. Unfortunately, the child welfare system has a poor record of family reunification. Once in care, children often linger in the system. In 2014, 53 percent of the children who left foster care had been in the system for twelve or more months.[93] The longer a child stays in care, the more likely he or she is to be moved from one foster placement to another, adding to disrupted relationships with siblings and relatives and the support of nonfamily members, such as teachers, coaches, religious leaders, and friends, increasing the risks of negative social and emotional outcomes.[94] Frequent changes in caseworkers, judges, and legal representation also interfere with the child's well-being and achievement of a permanent home.[14] For many children, the placement in foster care ends up as adverse community environment.

Adverse Community Environments

The original ACE survey focused on negative experiences within the family. As the survey has become widely known, practitioners also have identified adverse community environments that may disrupt child and adolescent development.[95] To best understand how both family and community experiences impact child and adolescent development, practitioners who use the ACE survey as a screening tool may consider asking questions related to the environment. Spotlight 5 illustrates community environments that may be included in such surveys. Whether these environments result in toxic stress depends on the frequency, duration, intensity, and context and the person's genetic makeup. Timing is also an important variable; there are times in a young person's life when he or she is more vulnerable to stress. As I discussed earlier, the brain is especially malleable to experiences during the first three years of life and during the teenage years.

Spotlight 5. Adverse Community Environments

Poverty

- Poor housing/homelessness
- Food insecurity
- Lack of mobility

Discrimination/harassment

- Racism
- Sexual orientation
- Religion
- Disability
- Place of birth

Community violence

- Gang involvement
- Threats from a romantic partner
- War

Loss of parent/caregiver

- Lingering in the child welfare system
- Deportation
- Death

Human trafficking

In the presence of supportive relationships and contexts, adverse events may be turned into tolerable stress. Youth practitioners can learn strategies that can turn toxic stress into tolerable stress for young people.

ACE scores do not define a whole child

Reflections

- Think about the background of the young people with whom you work. What adverse experiences have they experienced? How may their experiences impact their ability to learn and use social skills? What can you do to support them?
- Follow the blog at ACEs Too High at https://acestoohigh.com/aces-too-high-network/ to learn about adverse childhood experiences.

Explorations

- Watch the documentary *Paper Tigers: One high school's unlikely success story.*[96]
- Watch the documentary *Resilience: The biology of stress and the science of hope.*[97]

6

Brain Development Disrupted

The Amygdala: The Brain's Alarm System

The amygdala is the brain's alarm center that constantly scans the environment to meet our basic survival needs for safety, food, and sex.[98] It regulates emotions—especially fear, sadness, and anger—and generates internal emotional states and external expressions of these emotions.

The amygdala triggers automatic responses to perceived danger; that is, fight, flight, or freeze. During the first years of life, the amygdala also serves as a repository for emotional memories of fear, hurt, and threat. When a young person experiences intense stress, strong emotional memories are imprinted. Such intense early emotional experiences are stored in the form of sounds, smells, feelings, and emotions associated with the event. They are called *implicit memories*. Implicit memories also include procedural memories, which involve activities such as riding a bike or driving a car. Once such complex activities are learned, we do not use words to do them; we know how to do them without thinking. *Explicit memories*, on the other hand, are memories we recall and reflect on using words. Our earliest memories are called explicit memories.[99]

This section will explore how normal brain development may be disrupted and result in dysregulation of the stress response system, change gene expression, brain size and shape, and cause inflammation of the brain.

Fight, Flight, Freeze

Toxic stress during infancy and early childhood can leave the brain in a permanent stress-response mode. This state of stress makes the child respond in a hyper-vigilant and fearful manner.[100] An infant who is abused during the early months of life may show apathy, poor feeding, withdrawal, and failure to thrive. When the infant is under acute threat, the typical fight response to stress may change from crying (because crying did not elicit a response) to temper tantrums, aggressive behaviors, or inattention and withdrawal.[101] Toddlers may respond to intense stress with disengagement, detachment, apathy, and excessive daydreaming—the typical flight response. Some abused and neglected children learn to react to alarm or stress in their environment with immediate cessation of motor activity. This is a freeze response. As children grow older, the unresponsive freeze response may be perceived as oppositional or defiant by others.

Dysregulation of the Stress Response System

> States of autonomic hyperarousal are experienced as pain.[102]
>
> —Allan Schore

The body's stress response system is activated when a person experiences anger, fear, worry, anxiety, grief, loss, etc.[103] Under constant stress, the body does not recover to a state of equilibrium. It is as if the stress system never shuts off "even when no external threats exist, they are in a constant state of alarm."[104]

Let's explore what happens in the brain and the body when a person perceives a stressful situation through sight or sound. The amygdala compares the event with past experiences. If the event resembles past experiences that were painful or fearful, the amygdala triggers the person to react with thoughts and emotions like those that were activated during past events. In a sense, the amygdala convinces the person that all the dangerous conditions that existed in the past are currently present, even if they are not.

The autonomic system is signaled to respond to the situation. This system controls breathing, blood pressure, heartbeat, and dilation/constriction of key blood vessels and small airways in the lungs. The autonomic system consists of two subsystems. The first—the sympathetic system—gives the body a burst of energy to deal with the perceived danger, and the second system—the parasympathetic system—calms the body after the danger has passed. The first system acts like a gas pedal and the second like a brake.[105]

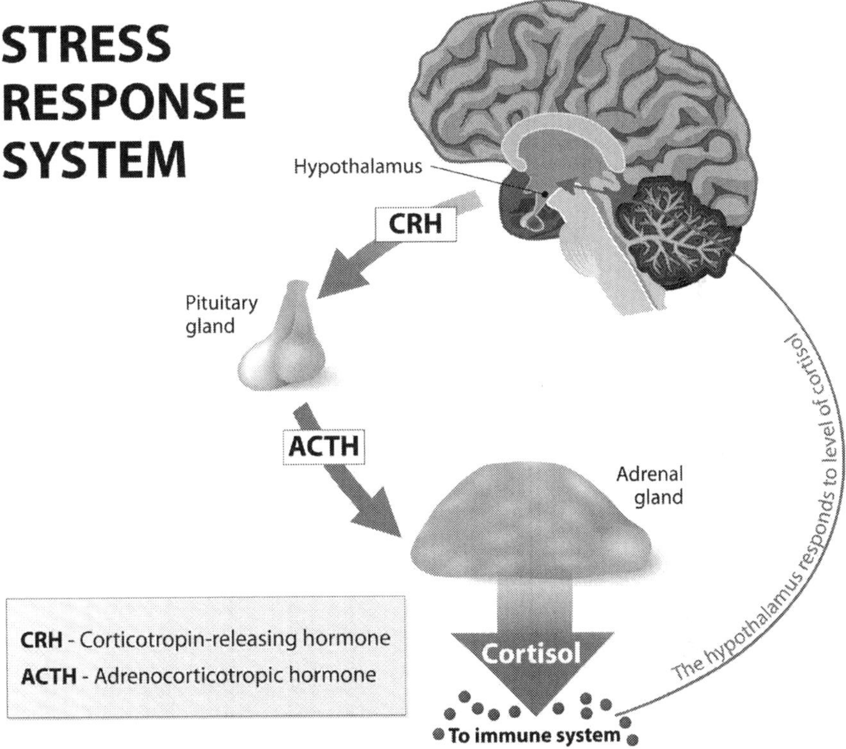

Figure 6. The stress response system

Let's dig a bit deeper into what happens. The sympathetic system signals the adrenal glands to release a hormone into the bloodstream that increases the heart rate and sends more blood to the muscles, heart, and other organs. Thus, we breathe faster and send more oxygen to the brain, which, in turn, alerts all our senses to be on guard. Simultaneously, adrenaline triggers the release of blood sugar (glucose) and fats from temporary storage sites in the body, giving the body more energy. As the initial flow of adrenaline decreases, the hypothalamus activates the second component of the stress system—the HPA axis (hypothalamus, pituitary gland, and adrenal glands). The HPA axis relies on hormonal signals to keep the sympathetic system active, keeping the gas pedal down. If the danger persists, the hypothalamus releases a hormone called corticotrophin (CRH stands for corticotrophin-releasing hormone), which travels to the pituitary gland, where another hormone, called ACTH (adrenocorticotropic), is released. This hormone travels to the adrenal glands, where cortisol is released to help the body to stay on high alert. When the threat lessens, so does the cortisol level. The parasympathetic system—the brake—dampens the stress response.[106]

In a fully developed brain, the prefrontal lobes serve as the brakes for surges in the amygdala. As we discussed earlier, the prefrontal lobes undergo major integration during the teenage years and are among the last to develop. Therefore, young people's brakes are not very effective.

Emotional Hijacking and Amygdala War

> Faced with a range of challenging behaviors, caregivers have a tendency to deal with their frustrations by retaliating in ways that uncannily repeat the children's early trauma.[107]
>
> —Bessel van der Kolk

When fully developed and integrated, the prefrontal lobes analyze our perceptions more thoroughly, sort out the details, and dampen or override signals from the amygdala in situations where we are not really at risk. While the prefrontal lobes are more accurate in their assessment of the situation, they are much slower to activate than the amygdala. For children and youth, the amygdala often activates the body's alarm system and short-circuits the prefrontal lobes' ability to evaluate the situation. Daniel Goleman called this emotional hijacking, a state where a person is neurologically impaired and cannot think straight.[108] When a person is emotionally hijacked, the mind and the body tend to become locked into a recurring pattern of the amygdala's emotional arousal, flooding the person with stress hormones, irrational fear, anxiety, or anger. These internal reactions often trigger repeated unhealthy and ineffective patterns of speech and action that can be harmful and even disastrous to a person's social relationships.

Young people who experience chronic and unpredictable stress are at high risk for emotional hijacking, resulting in pain-based behaviors. In these situations, they often react by fighting verbally and physically, destroying property, or running away. In some situations, adult supporters become emotionally hijacked themselves, resulting in an amygdala war.[109] Nick Long described this as a dance of disturbance that continues until at least one of the two parties disengages.[110] Sometimes, the conflict continues long after the event, and the young person becomes a prisoner of hate.[111]

Describing troubled emotions as pain is more than a figure of speech. When we say we have hurt feelings, it is literally true. Researchers found that physical and social pain operate in similar ways in the brain. Brain scans show that being excluded or rejected by others triggers feelings of distress and a burst of activity in the part of the brain that registers physical pain.[112]

Epigenetics

All experiences, whether positive or negative, leave chemical signatures on our genes. These signatures can be short-lived or long lasting and affect whether genes are turned on or off. Changes in gene expression are called epigenetics.[113] Chronic and unpredictable stress may produce a permanent state of fight-or-flight in the brain, and chemical markers may silence the genes that are supposed to regulate the stress response system throughout life. A study of fifty-six children with a history of child abuse found that genes involved in stress management were changed and put the children on constant alert. Thus, they misunderstood "normal" behavior as threatening and had difficulty with transitions. The long-term consequences of such epigenetic changes include anxiety, depression, and chronic physical problems, like heart disease and type II diabetes.[114]

Epigenetic changes also may help explain why adults who grew up with inadequate nurturance and experiences are often unable to nurture their own children. It is likely that the lack of nurturance the adults received silenced the genes that suppressed oxytocin—often called the love hormone—and instead turned on other genes that increased stress hormones.[115] Since brain development depends on brain to brain interactions with primary caregivers, epigenetics can help youth practitioners understand why harsh, abusive, and neglectful parenting run in families. Researchers continue to explore how genes are altered by adverse experiences.[116]

Changes to Brain Size and Shape

About 170,000 Romanian children lived in seven hundred overcrowded, barren, rundown state-operated orphanages at the collapse of Ceausescu's oppressive regime in 1989. The consequences of deprivation and neglect are described by Nelson, Fox, and Zeanah in their book *Romania's Abandoned Children.*[117] The children experienced an absence of human contact, social connections, stimulation, and comfort and were fed and changed in an assembly-like fashion. For most, the experience was devastating, resulting in poor attachment formation, developmental delay, poor physical development, and antisocial behavior. With limited serve-and-return experiences and other forms of communication, language and vocabulary development were impaired for many. Electroencephalograms (EEGs) were used to compare brain activity of never-institutionalized Romanian children to institutionalized children.[118] The latter group showed a markedly lower brain activity.

In a large study, participants who had been exposed to repeated and chronic stress were found to have smaller gray-matter volume in key prefrontal and limbic regions, the areas involved in regulating stress, emotion, reward, and impulse control.[119] A smaller gray-matter volume simply means that the people in the study had fewer neurons, as compared to people who had not been exposed to high levels of stress. As a result, it might be more challenging for these individuals to manage future stressful events. They also might be at increased risk for a future stressful and adverse life and at higher risk for stress-related mental and physical health outcomes.

Brain Inflammation

Nerve cells (neurons) and glial cells (glia) are the two major types of cells present in the brain. For many years, glial cells were thought to support only the activities of neurons. Glial cells were described as primarily serving a garbage removal function, including the removal of cell debris, foreign substances, and cancer cells to maintain a correct chemical concentration around neurons. Recent advances in neuroscience have established that microglia—a special form of glial cells—serve as the main defense in the immune system. Glial cells also are essential in the pruning of neural synapses and have a role in scanning the environment to detect danger or safety. When we are faced with stress, they may trigger chemicals that lead to inflammation of the brain.[120]

In a healthy brain, microglia regulate the number of neurons the cortex needs.[121] Under extreme stress, microglia can trigger excessive pruning in areas involved in executive functioning, such as reasoning and impulse control. McCarthy explained that microglia can encapsulate and destroy dying neurons, "but in other cases microglia are destroying healthy neurons and, in that case, it is more like murder."[122] She compares the brain to a stressed muscle that has lost its tone and is withering away. In the brain, the loss of gray and white matter can contribute, later in life, to depression, anxiety, schizophrenia, and Alzheimer's disease.

Positive, Tolerable, and Toxic Stress

Ongoing chronic and unpredictable stress activates the stress response system, with the possibility of causing damage to both mental and physical health. The more negative experiences a person has in childhood, the more likely he or she is to have developmental delays, learning problems, difficulty with impulse control, and early onset of health problems, such as diabetes, substance abuse, depression, suicide attempts, and heart disease. Young people may react with anger outbursts or feel numb, disconnected, and unable to trust peers and adults.

Stress affects each person differently. Experiences that disrupt healthy development and cause long-term difficulties with learning, relationships, behavior, and health problems for one person may be tolerable to another.

The impact of stress can be buffered by genetics, caring relationships and supportive ecologies. In summary, it is not events themselves that determine how a person is affected; rather, it is the effect the events have on the person's stress response system. The body's responses to activation of the stress response system fall into three distinct categories of stress: positive, tolerable, and toxic.[123]

Spotlight 6. Stress Influences Developmental Outcomes

Positive Stress	
Brief increases in heart rate, mild elevations in stress hormone levels	Important to development; often leads to new experiences; an opportunity for the brain to "stretch" and increase capacity
Tolerable Stress	
Serious temporary stress, buffered by supportive relationships and inner strengths	Potentially disruptive to development
Toxic Stress	
Chronic, unpredictable, and unresolved stress in the absence of protective relationships	Disrupts brain architecture; increases the risk of stress-related physical and mental illness

Positive stress is short-lived, and even though it may cause hormone levels and heart rate to increase, it often supports healthy development. It can result from making an oral presentation, performing in a play, or asking a person out on a date.

Tolerable stress can result from not fitting in at school, losing a parent or significant other, an accident, or a natural disaster. Provided the young person is surrounded by supportive adults in a safe environment, healthy development can be fostered and maintained.

Toxic stress can result from prolonged experiences of abuse, neglect, substance abuse, domestic and community violence, poverty, and racial discrimination. While such events are toxic to many young people, supportive relationships can buffer the person against long-term damage.

When young people are surrounded by supportive relationships and "good-fit" environments, they are on the way "to properly build the systems in the brain that connect reward, pleasure, and human-to-human interactions."[124] If the person's ecology is unsafe and lacks attuned, loving adults, and caregivers are inconsistent, inattentive, chaotic, ignorant, abusive, or neglectful, it can be a source of stress that disrupts the child's development.

Stressful events in any part of children's life space cause ripple effects throughout their environment and may result in psychoemotional pain. Pain is a sensory and emotional experience that cannot be understood based on the intensity of the stressful event alone. Even severe distress can become tolerable in a culture of caring human relations. However, stress experienced in the absence of human understanding often produces unbearable pain.

Reflections

- Think of a time when your amygdala hijacked you. How did you react? Reflect on how you would react if it happened today.
- What warning signs do you have that let you know you are about to be amygdala hijacked?
- Reflect on how you can support a young person who is experiencing an amygdala hijacking.
- Think of a young person with whom you work, and identify three ways you can help that person turn toxic stress into tolerable stress.

Explorations

- Listen to Nadine Burke Harris's TED Talk, "How Childhood Trauma Affects Health across a Lifetime."[125]
- Read *Childhood Disrupted: How Your Biography Becomes Your Biology, and How You Can Heal* by Donna Jackson Nakazawa.[126]
- Read *Helping Children Succeed: What Works and Why* by Paul Tough.[127]

PART III

Intentional Responsive Adult Practices

7

Creating Intentional Relationships

Growing "Weller than Well"

In the previous chapter, I discussed how toxic stress interrupts growth and development in young people. In part III of the book, I explore ten intentional responsive adult practices, beginning with four intentional capacity-building practices (chapters 7–10): (1) creating intentional relationships, (2) developing character strengths, (3) solidifying executive functions, and (4) tapping into culture and faith. Supporting a young person to strengthen each of these capacities can turn toxic experiences into tolerable events and set young people on a path toward well-being—what Karl Menninger called "weller than well."[128]

Children and young people who grow up with nurturing caregivers have repeated experiences of positive outcomes. Despite stress and adverse circumstances, their caregivers and environments mitigate these experiences in a reassuring way that reestablishes safety and nurtures the development of intellectual, social, emotional, and spiritual well-being. Young people who can adapt, cope, change, experience joy and fulfillment, and pursue goals and dreams in the face of adversity are growing "weller than well." When their inner resources and external supports are strong, children and youth are liberated from overwhelming psychosocial stress and pain. They can think about themselves and their world in positive ways and feel good about who they are and what they can accomplish in life. Well-being is not the absence of problems and challenges; rather, it is a way to achieve positive outcomes despite challenges. Well-being does not mean that stress is absent or should be avoided. To the contrary, science has demonstrated that human motivation peaks when people take on tasks at the edge of their comfort zones and current abilities. Nicholas Hobbs called this just manageable difficulties.[129]

Adults can support young people in growing weller than well through supportive relationships and by nurturing their character strengths and executive functions and responding to their culture and faith. Wrapped in support, youth can meet the five universal growth needs identified earlier, which resonate with these statements:

- I have a positive and supportive network of adults and peers.
- I achieve goals, take on challenges, and find solutions.
- I manage my emotions and actions to get positive results.
- I contribute and make a difference to others and the community.
- I have hope for the future and live a purposeful life.

The Need to Belong

> My humanity is caught up, is extricably bound up in yours. We belong in a bundle of life. A person is a person through others. A person is a person through another person.[130]
>
> —Archbishop Desmond Tutu

Positive and caring relationships with other people are the core of the human experience. Youth development, resilience, and well-being are rooted in relatedness. As social beings, humans experience their values, strengths, and emotions in relation with others. The concept of Ubuntu—deeply imbedded in some African cultures, particularly South Africa—captures the profound nature of relatedness as the "essence of being human." It is within their experience of relatedness that young people progress, learn, survive, hurt, struggle, meet their needs, cope with stress, increase their strengths, and thrive.

The ability to develop and maintain strong, stable interpersonal relationships is key to bouncing back from adverse experiences and to developing well-being.[131] The authors of a classic study on the need for belonging concluded,

"The desire for interpersonal attachment may well be one of the most far-reaching and integrative constructs currently available to understand human nature."[132] Children who have experienced toxic stress are often reluctant to form and sustain relationships with adults because their stress was at the hands of the people who were supposed to protect them. Youth practitioners must be intentional and diligent in providing these children with experiences that can help them to bond and develop relationships. Such experiences should be engaging and dynamic, activating the social synapse, the "medium through which we are linked together into larger organisms such as families, tribes, societies, and the human species as a whole."[133]

Relatedness and Attachment

Relatedness is achieved through interactions with people, animals, a higher power, spiritual beings, and the land. With good-enough parenting and experiences, relatedness is carried within the young person as a powerful internal growth resource.[134] It extends in a reciprocal fashion to others, like an intricate web spun around the individual. Over time, people form experienced-based relationship models that determine their anticipations, behaviors, and emotions in future interactions with other people, including teachers, friends, partners, colleagues, and others. These interactions determine how they think, feel, behave, and connect with people. Traditionally, relationship models have developed from interactions in the home, school, and community. Today, relationships extend through the internet, where people may be connected to hundreds of other people across the world.

Attachment pioneers John Bowlby and Mary Ainsworth identified two broad relationship or attachment models: secure and insecure.[135] Secure attachment promotes flexibility, self-understanding, and the ability to easily and flexibly connect with others. Insecure attachment is characterized by rigidity and poor or distorted self-understanding, often resulting in poor connections with others. Insecure attachment is divided into four subcategories: avoidant, ambivalent, disorganized, and reactive, each with distinct features.

Relatedness provides the life blood for human development. Young people thrive when they are wrapped in trusting, meaningful relationships with

adults and peers. For many indigenous children and youth, this extends to ancestors, the land, and the spiritual realm. For young people who believe in a God or a higher power, relatedness extends into the spiritual realm.

Stable, Caring, and Supportive Relationships

Stable, caring, and supportive relationships are essential to young people's development, learning, and flourishing. Research and folk wisdom unequivocally indicate that a high-quality relationship between an adult and a child is the strongest asset for positive development, resilience, and well-being.[136] Positive relationships buffer young people from engaging in high-risk behaviors (e.g., tobacco, alcohol, illicit drug usage).[137] Research also has shown that the length of relationships matter. Relationships lasting more than one year yield the best results.[138] Simply put, the longer a relationship lasts, the better. Unfortunately, it is also evident that unexpected termination of a relationship can have harmful effects on a child's development.[139]

Psychologist Peter L. Benson, who was the CEO/president of the Search Institute, observed that American schools, after-school programs, and other youth programs abruptly sever young people's relationships with adults.[140] Teachers, youth practitioners, and coaches often stay a year or less with young people! Add to this the high mobility of many families, and it is obvious that young people are challenged to have lasting relationships with supportive adults. As a matter of fact, 40 percent of young people report feeling lonely.[141]

Secure, lasting, and caring relationships are important to young people's development. Every young person needs at least one adult who is deeply interested in his or her well-being and who is willing to be there for the child or youth under all circumstances. Urie Bronfenbrenner noted that every child needs at least one adult who is irrationally crazy about him or her.[142] But one is not enough! Young people do better with a network of adults who provide different types of support and guidance. John Seita, who grew up in the foster care system, said that each kid needs a fan club of adults who can support and advocate for him or her in different ways.[143]

The critical factor is not merely the existence of a relationship but the responsive and interactive nature of that relationship. Unresponsive, indifferent, oppressive, or reactive relationships lack the nurturing capacity that is necessary for growth and is critical to well-being in stressful circumstances. When a person perceives a harmful event, attack, or threat, the brain's alarm system is triggered to compare the situation with past experiences to determine the threat level. When the brain determines a threat, real or perceived, the fight-flight-or-freeze response is activated. When young people experience an amygdala hijack, a trusting, supportive adult can help the them regulate their emotions until they can calm their emotional brains and engage their thinking brains. This coregulation has been compared to the support an air traffic controller provides to pilots during takeoff and landings.[144]

Caring and supportive relationships begin in the family, but strong relationships with nonfamily adults (such as neighbors, providers of early care and education, teachers, youth workers, social workers, counselors, and coaches) are just as important. Youth practitioners often fill that supportive role and provide advice, assistance, support, empathy, and respect for a period or throughout a young person's life. They help young people problem-solve and navigate paths to reach their aspirations for a good life.

An abundance of literature from the fields of education, psychology, social work, and mental health has documented that relationships matter. However, the literature is largely absent on the operationalization and description of the core elements and actions that promote youth/adult relationships. I will highlight three relationship frameworks that provide guidelines for best practices. One describes youth/adult relationships from the viewpoint of young people; the second is based on the perceptions of adult leaders in youth empowerment programs; and the last is on focus groups with youth, parents, educators, youth workers, and others.

Seven Habits of Caring Relationships

In 2003, Scott Birmingham and I interviewed twenty-three young people in four residential treatment centers in Virginia and Michigan about their perceptions of the characteristics of caring adults.[145] The interviews yielded the seven habits of caring relationships that are illustrated below.

Table 3. Seven habits of caring relationships

Habits	Actions	Beliefs
Trust	Doing what you say you are going to do	I'm accountable to the young people I serve.
Attention	Putting the young person at the center of concern	Children and youth are valuable and worthy.
Empathy	Seeing the world through the young person's eyes	There are many versions to the same story.
Availability	Making time for children and youth a top priority	Young people are important and worth an investment of my time and energy.
Affirmation	Saying positive things to and about a young person and meaning it	All young people have positive qualities and constructive behaviors that can be acknowledged.
Respect	Giving young people a say in decisions which affect them	Feelings are valid and young persons are the best experts on themselves.
Challenge and Support	Holding young people accountable for their actions without blaming and being a role model	Young people must learn self-regulation, and those who teach them must practice what they teach.

The young people conveyed that caring adults serve as a protective factor and strengthen their resilience as they work to bounce back from adversity. The young people affirmed the importance of adults cultivating caring relationships with them. Adults demonstrate that they care by having high expectations of young people and supporting their participation in activities that afford opportunities for success. The participants expressed that adults who are available to them and who are accepting, supportive, understanding, and interested in their development make all the difference.

Throughout my work, I have used the seven habits of caring relationships as a road map for reflection and skill development for myself and for youth practitioners who seek a positive impact on the lives of challenging youth.

Adult Roles in Youth Empowerment Programs

Researchers gathered information through interviews, observations, and discussions with leaders in youth programs to identify best practices in community-based youth programs.[146] They identified six dimensions of adult roles: (1) putting youth first; (2) raising the bar for youth performance; (3) creating space and making things happen; (4) being in relationships; (5) exerting influence, control and authority; and (6) connecting with the broader community.

Table 4. Adult roles in youth empowerment programs

Dimensions	Examples
Putting youth first	Making youth participation and engagement a priority. Valuing, respecting, and acknowledging youth. Recognizing the learning potential of both success and failure.
Raising the bar for youth performance	Setting and communicating high expectations for youth. Providing opportunities for youth to develop and practice leadership skills.
Creating the space and making things happen	Providing administrative and logistic support and structure. Making it fun.
Being in relationships	Being open and available and listening to youth. Role-modeling. Nurturing, protecting, and defending youth.
Exerting influence, control, and authority	Setting boundaries and monitoring youth behaviors. Keeping youth on task. Exerting influence and intervening to encourage youth interaction, enforce discipline, foster diversity, and increase youth potential.
Communicating and connecting with the broader community	Creating communication and support networks. Mobilizing resources. Reaching out to the community.

The framework of adult roles in community programs shares many of the findings of the seven habits of caring relationships described above. Common themes include adults listening and respecting young people, providing guidance, having high expectations, setting boundaries, and being role models. Adult leaders, however, experienced their roles with young people as more than caring. They identified the importance of creating opportunities for the youth voice and involvement in decisions within the program, allowing young people to use their potential and leadership and learn to take responsibility. Through purposeful program design, adults also create the space for youth to explore and try out new skills, build their personal and collective capacities, and experience both success and mistakes within a safe environment. Finally, adults in the study identified the importance of reaching out to the community to advocate for young people and share how youth can contribute to the community. The community outreach role also involves finding and soliciting resources to support the development of young people.

Developmental Relationships

The developmental relationships framework is the result of extensive research completed by the Search Institute that involves focus groups, review and analysis of existing research, and feedback from youth professionals and practitioners.[147]

Table 5. Developmental relationships framework

Elements	Actions	Definitions
Express Care	Be dependable. Listen. Believe in me. Be warm. Encourage.	Be someone I can trust. Really pay attention when we are together. Make me feel known and valued. Show me you enjoy being with me. Praise me for my efforts and achievement.
Challenge Growth	Expect my best. Stretch. Hold me accountable. Reflect on failures.	Expect me to live up to my potential. Push me to go further. Insist I take responsibility for my actions. Help me learn from my mistakes and setbacks.
Provide Support	Navigate. Empower. Advocate. Set boundaries.	Guide me through hard situations and systems. Build my confidence to take charge of my life. Defend me when I need it. Place limits to keep me on track.
Share Power	Respect me. Include me. Collaborate. Lead me.	Take me seriously and treat me fairly. Involve me in decisions that affect me. Work with me to solve problems and reach goals. Create opportunities for me to take action and lead.
Expand Possibilities	Inspire. Broaden my horizons. Connect.	Inspire me to see possibilities for my future. Expose me to new ideas, experiences, and places. Introduce me to more people who can help me grow.

The developmental relationships framework provides the most current and complete operationalization of relationships and can be used by nonfamily adults as a map to deliberately form and develop relationships with young people in a variety of settings. It applies to all young people, including those who have experienced adversity in life.

"Developmental relationships are characterized by reciprocal human interactions that embody an enduring human attachment, progressively more complex patterns of joint activity, and a balance of power that gradually shifts from the developed person in favor of the developing person."[148]

Developmental relationships are the critical components of interventions across child and youth programs. When developmental relationships are present, child-serving programs produce the desired positive outcomes, and when they are absent or weak, interventions are less effective.[149]

Relationship Building in Action

Can We Be Best Friends?

Meghan Ellis, a teacher in Virginia, shared how she developed a relationship with one of her students.[150]

> Towards the end of the school year, I learned that Charlotte would be in my class next year. In third grade, she had had increasing difficulties with relationships, self-regulation, and taking directions from adults. She had deteriorated after Christmas, when her home life changed.
>
> Honestly, I was apprehensive about having her in my class, as I had heard her behavior could be quite destructive, but I was determined to give her my unbiased best effort. I prepared during the summer by taking the *i*RAP course, reading a few books, and researching the effects of trauma online. I had a tentative plan for the school year that focused on developing an intentional relationship with

her. I knew that Charlotte would have to trust me before we could work on her IEP goals related to self-regulation and academics.

The first two days of school went smoothly, but on the third, she had her first meltdown during resource. Administration handled the situation, but I was able to sit with her toward the end and calming-down time as we kicked a ball back and forth on the office floor. For the next few days, I observed how her voice changed and eyes dilated when her anxiety increased, leading toward a meltdown.

The following week I was called to the auditorium. Charlotte had another episode and was currently standing on the table, causing quite the scene. When she saw me, with administration trailing behind, she ran to the corner behind a trashcan. I decided to take this situation into my own hands and see it through to the end. I proceeded to sit on the floor, beside the trashcan for twenty minutes, not asking questions, just letting her get out her frustration and anger. We eventually moved from the floor while she moved throughout the auditorium, attempting to destroy anything in her path but still talking for about an hour. I was given the opportunity to go back to class but felt it was important to see Charlotte's full range of emotions during an episode and for her to know I wasn't leaving her. With the guidance of administration, I saw the episode coming to an end. Her voice turned back to her normal tone, and her eyes were less dilated. She seemed emotionally and physically exhausted and had slowly moved from a chair a few feet away to sitting on my lap like a small child.

After this, Charlotte and I began to have lunch together in my classroom and play Monopoly. Slowly but surely, I could tell she started to feel safe with me. During small talk about the game, she began to give me glimpses into the things that bothered her. I followed up and asked what she was feeling about what she had said. She usually answered, and we then returned to the game.

My class has recess after lunch, and one day Charlotte asked if she could stay with me instead of going out. I now had an hour and a half with her every day and no planning time whatsoever. But we had time to build our relationship through games, talking, and writing to each other in her dialogue journal. After several weeks, she asked if we could be best friends. I said, "Of course we can. If we are best friends, you will also have to hear about my bad days and if I am stressed out." She said, "That's OK. You deal with me all the time."

During class, she worked on an independent study that we would meet to check and discuss, but I let her complete it at her own pace, which gave her a sense of control. The closer our relationship developed, the smoother things went in class.

Occasionally, Charlotte went outside to play with a friend who had shown a genuine desire for a friendship. I knew at this point that we were making progress with her ability to create relationships. Next, we asked the friend, Ellie, to join us in a game of UNO. I played one game with them, and then they played without me while I got some work done. When they got into an argument about one of the rules, Charlotte suggested they should stop playing because "it is bad for our relationship to argue." I told her that they needed to work out their disagreement because it is OK for friends to disagree—and they did, luckily with much success! They continue to play together regularly.

By December, we began inviting her friend and other adults (her counselor, my co-teacher, and the math teacher) to have lunch with us. Charlotte talks a bit with them if I am there but still doesn't like to leave the room without me.

Some people think Charlotte may be getting too attached to me. I disagree; I want her to have a strong relationship with someone whom she feels safe with and whom she can trust. Once she has one, she can begin to build relationships with other adults and children. She will be in elementary school for another year and a half, and I am going nowhere. And after that, I will still be with her.

Charlotte and I continue to work on our relationship, and I am beginning to expand her circle of support—to build the Charlotte Fan Club. She is beginning to see and feel what a calm, happy school day feels like. Now that she feels safe with me and knows that she has a safe place to go to each day, we can begin working on her self-regulation and fill her toolbox with strategies she can use when she feels her anxiety and anger become overwhelming. I have always held classroom community and strong relationships in high priority, but Charlotte has proven just how impactful intentional relationships can be.

The Healing Power of Relationship and Jazz[151]

Tabitha was born in 2015. I know her parents, Kevin and Jackie, love her and will do everything in their power to challenge her to pursue greatness through failure and success. They will give her opportunities to make her own decisions (while considering the impact on others) and teach her to be generous.

Fifteen year earlier, Kevin's life was in shambles, and he sought me out just a couple of days before Christmas. Here is what he shared: "My mom was sixteen when she had me. She couldn't really take care of me because she was so young. The first couple of years, she often left me and my two-years-older brother alone for hours while she went out partying. She started doing drugs and was in out and out of prison. I stayed with my grandmother and my uncle, but it was Granny who raised me. When Mom got out of prison, she would come to live with us. It was always chaotic. Granny and Mom yelled and screamed at one another most of the time. When they wouldn't calm down, my uncle started yelling and throwing things at them. If they didn't stop yelling, he would strike out at anyone in reach. He was very violent. When I was about seven, he began sexually molesting me when Granny was out. He said it was our secret and that he would kill me if I told anyone. When I was about nine, I was out of control in school and at home. I got into fights with other kids at school and in the community. I hit teachers, and one time I trashed the principal's office. My grandma was so frail. She couldn't handle me. So I was put in foster care."

Kevin lived with six different foster families over the next five years. He continued to escalate his behaviors and was then sent to the residential program, where I served as the director. During the first several months, it was difficult for staff to understand and support Kevin in managing his behaviors. It appeared that the harder staff tried to connect with him, the more he pushed back. Explosive outbursts of verbal and physical aggression toward staff, peers, and property were daily occurrences. It seemed we were not able to understand his pain. One morning after another explosive episode, the night staff asked me to talk with him. Kevin reluctantly followed me to my office and let me know that "I'm f**** not goin' to talk to you 'bout nothin'." I had some jazz music playing, and Kevin sat down. I accepted that he was not planning to talk with me, so I sat down without saying anything. After a while Kevin broke the silence and said, "Who's that playing?" "Art Blakey," I responded. It was obvious that Kevin was beginning to relax. After fifteen to twenty minutes of listening to jazz and not talking, Kevin said he was ready to go to school. As we walked to the school, we "ran into" the night staff, and Kevin mumbled, "Sorry, man." ... Over the next several months, Kevin and I had jazz time three or four times a week. We listened to Miles Davis, Coleman Hawkins, Thelonious Monk, Charlie Parker, Charles Mingus, Art Tatum, and many others. Sometimes we just listened, and sometimes we talked. The staff members who worked with Kevin observed that he became better and better at regulating his emotions. He had fewer and fewer explosive episodes, and within the next eight to nine months, we found a foster mother who took Kevin into her home.

Kevin lived with Ms. Jones for almost three years. She cared tirelessly for the foster youth in her home and treated them as her own children. Shortly after Kevin graduated from high school, he turned eighteen. Even though Ms. Jones told him he could stay with her, he left to seek out his family, as do many other youth in foster care. The next few years were turbulent as he tried to find support and stability from his family. He had some good moments, particularly with Granny.

The time he sought me out a few days before Christmas, his life was in shambles. He was broke, homeless, unemployed, and had a six-month-old daughter, Aretha, whose mother was seventeen years old. Kevin and the mother had lived together for a few months, but it didn't work out, and

Aretha was now raised by the maternal grandmother. It looked like Aretha was on a path to mirror Kevin's life.

After I caught up on Kevin's life, he asked how my two children were doing. I had often brought them to work for social events while he was in the program, and my son and Kevin had talked several times. Now, in the middle of his own pain, he was genuinely interested in hearing about my children. We returned to Kevin's life. He had no plans for the next few hours or days, much less anything after that. I suggested that we listen to some jazz to let it inspire us to come up with some ideas. We listened, talked, and agreed to call Ms. Jones but didn't reach her. We listened and talked some more. After a couple of hours, we reached Ms. Jones. She was elated to hear Kevin's voice and said his room was waiting for him. I drove him to Ms. Jones's home, where he was met with a warm smile and an embrace. She said, "I'm so glad you are home."

After the holidays, Kevin found work in a day care center. He has visited the residential program many times and talked with students in the program to give them hope for the future. His recipe is simple: relationships and jazz.

Kevin reconnected with Granny and took care of her until she passed. He has found a way to be with other family members and is actively involved in Aretha's life. Kevin was married in 2011 and had another daughter. I recently received a text message from him: "I am dancing with Tabitha to the tunes of Ben Webster." I was reminded of the healing power of jazz and relationships. I know Kevin, Tabitha, Aretha, and his wife will be fine.

Positive Peer Relations

Although supportive caregivers and youth practitioners are essential to young people's development, peers greatly impact each other's values and behaviors and the ways they strive to meet universal growth needs. Young people's health and educational outcomes are also strongly influenced by their peers. Positive peers support prosocial behavior, including engagement in school, homework completion, leisure activities, and hope for the future. Prosocial peers help protect one another from bullying and victimization and seek out support from adults when needed.

Peer relations are essential to understanding and navigating the ever-emerging life of their generation. Connecting and bonding with friends goes a long way to ensuring well-being and to becoming an independent and connected adult. As a result, young people have an inherent desire to talk with and listen to suggestions from their friends. It is one of the avenues to meeting their needs for belonging, helping others, and finding hope and purpose. As contemporaries they help one another by sharing experiences and changing the viewing of events. It helps them discover different solutions and pathways to meet their growth needs. Peers also can affirm to each other that they are not alone and can listen, offer acceptance, test values, and find solutions.

Knowing that peers are important, youth practitioners must develop skills to enlist young people in the helping process by inviting them to give advice to their peers. Though young people may have different suggestions than you, remind yourself that new ideas encourage curiosity, perspective, creativity, and independence. Doing so goes a long way to supporting them in meeting their psychosocial growth needs and provides a secure foundation for positive peer groups to develop.

The power of positive peers is often not included in discussions about relationships and their importance for children and youth who have experienced adversity. From middle childhood through the teenage years, young people increase the time they spend with peers. Peer group characteristics are diverse, though age and shared interests and activities contribute to young people's peer affiliations. Peer groups exist wherever young people gather—in schools, sports activities, after-school programs, online, and in the community at large.

Young people are typically associated with several peer groups. The frequency and depth of interactions with each group determine how peers are described, ranging from friends to associates, buddies, posse, or gang. For example, a young person may be connected to a small group or clique at school, while at the same time he or she is influenced by the overall climate or culture in the school and the young people with whom he or she associates in the community.

Young people spend the most time with those peers they feel are similar.[152] Youth who are engaged in school and value learning are likely to hang out with others with similar interests, while young people who struggle academically and are disconnected from school are likely to be lonely or be with kids like themselves. Young people who are disengaged in school are more likely to participate in antisocial and delinquent activities.

Adolescents who are well connected to their parents and other supportive adults continue to spend about the same amount of time talking one-on-one with their parents during the teenage years, while increasing the time spent with peers.[153] Young people who have experienced adversity are in double jeopardy because they tend to find and affiliate with peers like themselves. With broken relationships at home and friends with similar background, they lack the support of positive adults and peers.

Children and youth who have experienced adversity are often grouped in special classes at school, in alternative schools, and with other services meant to support them. Multiple studies have documented that many of these programs and services have unintentional effects. The influence of other young people with a history of trauma can lead to peer deviancy training; that is, instead of getting better, young people in the program end up reinforcing aggression, delinquency, and other antisocial behaviors in one another.[154] However, those programs that create a culture of respect and are well-structured and guided by positive youth development practices do not fall victim to peer deviancy training.[155] In other words, youth practitioners can facilitate the development of positive peer relations and positive peer cultures.

Most research related to creating positive peer cultures has been conducted using the term "school connectedness." The Centers for Disease Control and Prevention defines school connectedness as "the belief held by students that adults and peers in the school care about their learning as well as about them as individuals."[156] Four factors promote school connectedness: (1) adult support, (2) belonging to a positive peer group, (3) commitment to learning, and (4) a nurturing culture.[157]

Spotlight 7. School Connectedness

Young people who feel connected to school are less likely

- to engage in fighting, bullying, vandalism;[158]
- to smoke cigarettes, drink alcohol, or have sexual intercourse;
- to carry weapons, become involved in violence, or be injured from dangerous activities, such as drinking and driving or not wearing seatbelts;
- to have emotional problems, suffer from eating disorders, or experience suicidal thoughts or attempts;[159]
- to get involved with gangs.[160]

Young people who are connected to school and positive peer groups increase their regular school attendance, and they stay in school longer. They also improve their grades and test scores, and their rate of high school graduation.[161]

Developing Cultures of Respect

Youth practitioners can leverage the influence of peers to serve as a protective factor for disconnected youth who have experienced adversity. When adults facilitate the development of positive peers and peer groups, they create opportunities to meet the need for belonging and the benefits of relatedness.

Spotlight 8. Benefits of Positive Peers and Peer Groups

- Peers understand one another in a different way than adults do, and they provide the opportunity to test values, beliefs, opinions, behaviors, and the effectiveness of communication. Peers can give and receive feedback to create meanings, perceptions, and solutions, and interactions are a laboratory for discussion, problem solving, and negotiation.[162]
- Peer groups offer the opportunity to practice democracy.[163]
- Peer groups support healthy brain development.[164]

The development of a peer culture of respect begins with the youth practitioner facilitating the development of core expectations for the group. In my work with groups, I begin by introducing the simple—though complex and powerful—value that everyone is expected to help and be concerned with the well-being of others. Once the norm has been established, the adult can facilitate the group to explore whether interactions between group members are helpful or hurtful. This exploration is best facilitated by using an indirect approach, engaging and empowering group members to examine a multitude of interactions. For example, "Does Jamon have everyone's attention now?" or "Is the group ready to listen to what Jamon has to say?" rather than the directive statement, "Be quiet so you can hear what John has to say?"

Let me give another example: You notice a bruise over a kid's eye and ask what happened. He says it's a carpet burn he got from playing Blackout, a game that involves participants choking one another until one of them passes out. You find out that the game was played during English class while the teacher worked with a small group of students in an adjacent group room. What would you do, with respect to staff and students? You could conclude that the teacher did not provide sufficient supervision and is responsible for the event. Therefore, the teacher must be held accountable and will be expected to increase the level of supervision in the future. If you select this solution, the students likely will circumvent any preventive measures you put in place and will get the message that adults are responsible for their (the students') actions.

You could also decide that the students must learn to be responsible for their actions and call a group meeting to help the students understand that letting a peer pass out is hurtful. You could challenge the students' values and thinking and hold them responsible by letting them know that they engaged in the game because they did not care about each other. You might ask the group a series of questions: "Why didn't you see this coming? How could you have prevented it? How else has inattentiveness affected you in class? What can you do to get to know your group members better? What other activities can you do to meet your need for adventure and challenge?" In this way, you can hold the peer group responsible for their actions and challenge them to come up with solutions, rather than the adult doing the work for them.

In some situations, youth practitioners are oblivious to the negativity, intimidation, and hurtfulness that take place, as described above. More often, adults overlook or tolerate hurtful actions and rationalize that the kids are horseplaying. However, when youth practitioners do not address hurtful actions, young people get the message that helping is expected only some of the time. With intentional facilitation, however, young people can be enlisted to help and respect others.

Class Meetings

Class meetings at school are one of the best ways to develop a sense of community and to lay a foundation for belonging and a positive culture. The meeting typically lasts for twenty to thirty minutes and often is structured around building positive relationships, understanding and managing feelings, problem solving, and decision making.[165] School leaders support teachers by facilitating a schoolwide culture of respect. As a principal of Oak Grove-Bellemeade Elementary School in Richmond, Virginia, Jannie Laursen began each day with an affirmation of the school's values. Throughout the school day, teachers used the affirmation to facilitate discussions and problem solving with students.

I am a member of the Oak Grove-Bellemeade family.
I am the hope for our future.
I help others and maintain order.
I see possibilities!
I set high expectations for myself and others.
H-O-P-E
Hope for you, and hope for me!

Peer Relations and Peer Group Development in Action

Logan Cheers Me Up

Jamie Leech, a teacher in an inclusive classroom in Virginia, shared how she builds peer relations in her classroom.[166]

> I have been a teacher for seventeen years and have always felt it is important to build relationships in my classroom. Each day I pull the kids together in a circle for about fifteen minutes to develop relationships and a respectful classroom climate.
>
> I begin the circle time with a probing question that is relevant to the way my students interact with one another or to other issues that are related to their development or concerns. I may, for example ask, "What does it feel like when someone makes you feel you don't belong?" Rather than lecturing, I use think-pair-share. Each student has a little time to think about the question; then they pair and share their thoughts and feelings with one another. We end with sharing some examples with the whole class. Each day they pair up with a new person, so they get to know everyone in the classroom. At the end of the meeting, I ask if any of them have something else on their minds that they would like to share. A lot of hands always shoot up. As a student shares, others express how they can relate to that student's feelings, and they offer words of encouragements, empathy, and support.

Throughout the day I look for positive or negative interactions among my students. Before they go home, I pull them together and ask them to share examples of how others made them feel throughout the day. Their examples may guide the prompts I use the next day. Over time, the students develop trust, with me and with one another. They learn that we respect one another and that it is safe to talk about anything.

Several years ago, someone shared the book *How Full Is Your Bucket?*[167] with me. The book explains that we all have invisible buckets of water over our heads. Hurtful and negative actions can empty the buckets, so we always need to have our buckets refilled. All my students have a bucket, and I ask them to put a drop of encouragement or thanks into someone else's bucket each day. They can't wait to get their drops at the end of day! It is a great way to end the day. Parents have told me how much the drops mean to their children.

Since my whole school has daily meetings, we are paired up with other classes. My students have first-graders as buddies. We meet with them once a week to build friendship outside the class. For the first meeting, my kids had written letters, and the first-graders had made pictures. They talked about how the letters and pictures made them feel; it is a good way for my students to learn to help younger kids and for the first-graders to have role models.

I like to involve the parents too and have used an activity where I ask my students to interview a parent or another adult in the home about a person who has made a difference in his or her life. The student writes the story the adult told and then writes a story about someone who has made a difference in his or her own life. The adult writes a short comment about the experience, and the student brings the worksheet to school. One of my students wrote about a boy who had made a difference in his life. I was so surprised when I found out that he had written about another boy in my class—the student who was the hardest for me to reach. He had a long history of abuse and was becoming an abuser himself. I felt bad that I had overlooked that he was making friends in the classroom. It took one of my other students to point it out for me to see.

It's so important to make time to talk about what goes on inside you. I make anything that bothers a child a big deal. Nothing is too small to be talked about. The class meeting would be the last thing to go in my classroom.

Building a Schoolwide Culture

Neal Sarahan, codirector of Integral Flow in Texas, shared his experiences with building a culture of respect.[168]

> When we started a school for students with neurological differences twenty years ago, we had a mission: Shape our community to increase relationship development and executive functions. All of our students had experienced alienation or exclusion from a true learning community in one or more schools before joining us. Our students brought with them trauma borne of neurological differences, such as autism, seizure disorders, and Tourette's, and trauma from previous childhood experiences. Our school community had to grow trust by offering practices of relationship expansion, self-regulation, and ownership, based on the best executive functions possible.
>
> We began by meeting the students where they were, not by focusing on grade level or age standards. We knew that even with the best intentions and aspirations for a positive

learning community, students on the autism spectrum and with other social dislocations would not automatically adapt to a set of *rules*. We needed to have a governmental structure that was peer- and citizen-oriented and that did not depend too deeply on adult constraints and adult-generated rules. We didn't expect that students and faculty would meet expectations 100 percent of the time. Conflict should be expected and used to generate experiences that lead to developmental growth.

Believing that the highest order of governance includes the participation and consent of the governed, we organized groups of students and faculty to express their authentic hopes about what sort of community they wanted, how they wanted to be treated, and what they were willing to try to accomplish in their environment—a sort of Declaration of Rights and Responsibilities. Representatives from each group then came together to merge the group intentions. With lots of back and forth, a 100 percent consensus emerged. It took a lot of collaboration and perspective-taking to arrive at consensus—remember that this process was with students neurologically inclined to have perspective-sharing and compromise deficits. Sometimes it was contentious to find agreement. We asked that each objection be joined with a rationale *and* an invitation to adjustment. They could not just say no.

It took some incentives to move the process along. In our case, there was a logical connection between the consensual frame and the turning on of normal community functions. Until we had our core values and procedures, we did not turn on clubs, field trips, free lunches, or dances.

Once we had agreement, everyone—students and faculty—were held to the intentions. We developed a process for student leaders, with faculty support, to work through situations where the intentions were not followed. If someone felt that intentions had not been met, the person would be referred to the student-led discipline council for either mediation or restoration. Breakdowns did occur and were anticipated. Learners and faculty did disturb the community by repeatedly interrupting class, insulting others, being violent, or in my case, for example, by saying something in public that would have been better said in private. (Not humiliating others was one of our core intentions!) In general, community broke down for two reasons: communication misunderstandings and self-centeredness—when a person put his or her own needs in front of the needs of the community. Any person in the community could refer the situation—called a strike or a mediation request—to the discipline council. The function of the discipline council was not to punish but to support the person to rejoin the community.

Some situations were beyond the control of the discipline council and were referred to the adults. By example, a student hacked the school's computer system and assigned it to the Center for SETI Research for extraterrestrials. Mostly, the adults were needed to deal with social regulation difficulties, such as a student going off medications, student violence, or family chaos. We learned that students living with trauma express that trauma in ways that some discipline councils are not equipped to handle.

After a year of operation, we assumed (incorrectly) that the constitution would just carry over into the next year. We were wrong. Eight students did not consent to the "old" core values. We held a constitutional convention, and after six weeks we had version 2. Among other changes, the "discipline council" became the "leadership council." We provided a youth leadership program where leaders trained to become peer mediators. The student leaders focused more on their positive roles than on "policing" the community. In each year to follow, the constitution was reexamined and rewritten. Changes occurred. The leadership council became responsible for representing the community wishes, as well as mediating conflict. They suggested quality improvements to the justice system, polled the learners for field-trip structure, made dances more inclusive, advocated successfully for school-uniform changes, and assured representation to all.

Constant and intentional practice is necessary to keep ownership of the intentions. As with any other skill you want to master, intentional and frequent practice is necessary. If there weren't fifteen to twenty mediations a week, we instigated a process for ferreting out the conflicts that were not being expressed.

In our open enrollment program, new students were not assumed to have agreed to the governing structure. They were offered a cocoon period and were assigned a student guide to orient to the governing structure. They would not be expected to operate within the conflict resolution processes until they understood—and consented.

By being part of building a positive learning community, students took on their role as co-owners of their school culture.

Reflections

- Reflect on how you connect and develop relationships with kids. Share your insight with a colleague, and jointly expand your repertoire of connectibilities.

- Talk with a young person to learn how he or she knows that an adult supports his or her development; then reflect on your own practice.
- Reflect on how you build peer relations in your context.

Explorations

- Watch *Chad.*[169]
- Watch *Students Explain: Positive, Caring Relationships. Respect and Responsibility Modeled and Practices.* [170]
- Listen to Rita Pierson's TED Talk, "Every Kid Needs a Champion".[171]
- Watch *The Power of Relationships in the Lives of Youth.*[172]
- Seek out resources on class meetings, and develop a plan to institute class meetings with the students with whom you work.

8

Developing Character Strengths

Youth practitioners often work from a cause-and-effect model, referred to as the medical or the deficit-focused model. Within this model, practitioners first determine what a child's presenting problem is, then assign the problem a proper diagnosis, and finally begin to alleviate the problem. In the deficit-focused model, identification of mental disorders and educational disabilities is central. Disability labels are required to receive funding for mental health, educational, or social services, both from public agencies and private insurance companies. Practitioners use the vocabulary outlined in manuals and regulations to produce diagnoses. The Diagnostic and Statistical Manual of Mental Disorders and special education regulations are examples of protocols that are used to identify and communicate about a child's problem.[173]

Most practitioners, working from the deficit-focused model, also ask open-ended questions to solicit young people's strengths, talents, skills, and environmental resources. This informal approach to strength assessment, however, typically lacks a common language. In the absence of a well-defined vocabulary, children's strengths and resources often get lost in the detailed description of faults and deficits.

Focus on What's Strong, Not What's Wrong

> Having a common language for character strengths gives a practical way to discover and amplify how young people use them.

The second intentional responsive adult practice is to use the VIA Survey to name and develop young people's character strengths.[174] When young people discover their strengths and learn how to draw on them in the right amount in different situations, they can use them to pursue the outcomes they want. The VIA Institute on Character has shown that the intentional use of character strengths helps people manage and overcome problems, improve relationships, and enhance health and overall well-being.

Spotlight 9. Different Kinds of Strengths

Talents—what we do naturally well
Skills—what we train ourselves to do
Interests—our passions
Resources—our external supports
Values—what we internally hold dear
Character strengths—positive, trait-like capacities for thinking, feeling, and behaving in ways that benefit oneself and others

Youth practitioners must learn to identify the strengths that young people can mobilize to bolster their ability to cope with stress and to thrive. These capabilities include talents, skills, interests, values, resources, and character strengths. Humor, creativity, insight, independence, spirituality, perseverance, playing an instrument, caring for young children or the elderly, cooking, writing, a passion for the environment, having a "knack" for numbers, storytelling, and so forth are all examples that fall under the "strengths" umbrella. The influence of personal strengths can expand as the young person grows and develops and may be an added layer of protection against adversity.

What Are Character Strengths?

Ryan Niemiec, education director of the VIA Institute on Character, identifies character strengths as the driving force in our lives. He has suggested that "talents can be squandered, resources can be quickly lost, interests wane and change, skills diminish over time, but when all seems completely lost we still have our character strengths. When focused on, our character strengths crystallize and evolve and can integrate with other positive qualities to contribute to the greater good."[176]

Youth practitioners can leverage young people's character strengths to tip the scale toward positive outcomes. When youth practitioners support young people in naming and developing young people's strengths, they give them tools they can use as buffers during times of stress. This is more effective and more constructive than focusing on pathology and attempting to "fix" problems.[177] Recognizing and mobilizing young people's strengths[178]

- conveys respect and honors their struggles by seeing their behavior and the choices they make in the context of their challenges;
- shifts their self-image from "problemed youth" to "one who prevails";
- provides evidence of their capacity to face challenges in the past and that they can do so again; and
- uncovers and names strengths they used successfully in the past and identifies that they can be used again.

People around the world value similar strengths and virtues, although they are expressed and acted upon contextually. In the early 2000s, Chris Peterson and Martin Seligman set out to discover and identify these commonly shared strengths and virtues. Through extensive research over a three-year period, they identified six virtues and twenty-four character strengths (shown in Table 6) that are valued by people around the world, regardless of cultural, racial, or religious differences.[179]

They also developed a scientifically validated survey—the VIA Survey—to access a person's character strengths. The survey can be completed online at http://www.viacharacter.org. It is free and takes twenty to thirty minutes to complete. A special version is designed for youth aged ten to seventeen. The survey identifies a person's character strengths and gives practitioners and young people a "language of strengths" to use in their day-to-day interactions. Strengths give people energy and help them function authentically and at their best.

Table 6. Virtues and character strengths

Wisdom Cognitive strengths that entail the acquisition and use of knowledge				
Creativity	**Curiosity**	**Judgment**	**Love of Learning**	**Perspective**
Thinking of new and productive ways to conceptualize and do things	Taking interest in people and experiences for their own sake; openness to experience; finding subjects fascinating; exploring and discovering	Thinking things through; considering every point of view; not jumping to conclusions; weighing all/ considering new evidence; critical thinking	Mastering new skills and topics; deliberately seeking to add to what one knows	Wisdom; able to provide wise counsel to others; ways of looking at the world that makes sense to oneself and other people
Courage Emotional strengths that involve the exercise of the will to accomplish goals in the face of opposition, external or internal				
Bravery	**Perseverance**	**Honesty**	**Zest**	
Not shrinking from threat, challenge, difficulty, or pain; speaking up for what is right, even when there is opposition; acting on convictions, even if unpopular; being physically brave	Persistence, despite obstacles; finishing what one starts; taking pleasure in completing tasks	Authenticity; integrity; speaking the truth; presenting oneself in a genuine way, without pretense; taking responsibility for one's feelings and actions	Vitality, energy, enthusiasm; approaching life with excitement and energy; not doing things halfway or half-heartedly; living life as an adventure; feeling alive	

Humanity Interpersonal strengths that involve tending and befriending others				
Love	**Kindness**	**Social Intelligence**		
Valuing close relationships with others, those where sharing and caring are reciprocated; being close to people	Generosity, nurturance, care, compassion; doing favors and good deeds for others; helping others; taking care of them	Emotional intelligence; being aware of the motives and feelings of other people and self; knowing what to do to fit into different situations; knowing what makes other people tick		
Justice Civic strengths that underlie healthy community life				
Teamwork	**Fairness**	**Leadership**		
Citizenship, social responsibility, loyalty; working well and being a loyal team member; doing one's share	Treating people the same, according to notions of fairness and justice; not letting personal feelings bias decisions about others; giving everyone a fair chance	Encouraging a group to which one belongs to get things done while maintaining good relations; organizing group activities and seeing that they happen		
Temperance Strengths that protect against excess				
Forgiveness	**Humility**	**Prudence**	**Self-Regulation**	
Forgiving those who have done wrong; accepting the shortcomings of others; giving people a second chance; not being vengeful	Letting one's accomplishments speak for themselves; not regarding oneself as more special than others	Being careful about one's choices; not taking undue risk; not saying or doing things that may later be regretted	Self-control; regulating what one feels and does; being self-disciplined; controlling one's appetites and emotions	

Transcendence Strengths that forge connections to the larger universe and provide meaning				
Appreciation of Beauty and Excellence	**Gratitude**	**Hope**	**Humor**	**Spirituality**
Awe, wonder; noticing and appreciating beauty, excellence, and skilled performance in various aspects of life—from nature to art, math, science, and everyday experience	Being aware of and thankful for good things that happen; taking time to express thanks	Optimism; future-mindedness, future orientation; expecting the best in the future and working to achieve it; believing that good fortune can be brought about	Playfulness; liking to laugh and tease; bringing smiles to other people; seeing the light side	Faith, purpose; having coherent beliefs about the higher purpose and meaning of the universe; knowing where one fits within the larger scheme; having beliefs about the meaning of life that shape conduct and provide comfort

The VIA youth survey report ranks a person's twenty-four character strengths, from those that are expressed the most to those that are least used (Figure 7). This constellation of character strengths is unique to each person and are expressed in different contexts (e.g., at home, in school, in the community). People express their character strengths to different degrees, and all twenty-four strengths matter. Sometimes people believe that their lowest character strengths represent a deficit or a weakness. Not so. It simply means that the person does not draw on these strengths as frequently as on others. A person's top five or six character strengths are called his or her signature strengths. They are the core of a person—who the person really is—and, when used, energize the person and are recognized by family and friends.

Charissa Kline

1: Spirituality
Having coherent beliefs about the higher purpose and meaning of the universe; knowing where one fits within the larger scheme; having beliefs about the meaning of life that shape conduct and provide comfort.

2: Appreciation of Beauty & Excellence
Noticing and appreciating beauty, excellence, and/ or skilled performance in various domains of life, from nature to art to mathematics to science to everyday experience.

3: Forgiveness
Forgiving those who have done wrong; accepting others' shortcomings; giving people a second chance; not being vengeful.

4: Humor
Liking to laugh and tease; bringing smiles to other people; seeing the light side; making (not necessarily telling) jokes.

5: Kindness
Doing favors and good deeds for others; helping them; taking care of them.

6: Fairness
Treating all people the same according to notions of fairness and justice; not letting feelings bias decisions about others; giving everyone a fair chance.

Figure 7. Youth report: Ranking of character strengths

Character strengths can be over- or underused; a person should strive to balance the use of his or her strengths.[180] Two of my top character strengths are perseverance and curiosity. They have served me very well throughout the writing of this book and, due to some overuse, have driven me to continue to seek more information, which has delayed the completion of the manuscript. I have had to balance the overuse with one of my other signature strengths—perspective—to acknowledge that if I ever wanted to publish a book, I had to set a deadline to stop seeking more information.

The Aware-Explore-Apply Model

About ten years ago, we began administering the VIA Survey to students at Charterhouse School, where I served as the executive director. We explored the results with the students but could not find out how to support the students in developing their character strengths. A couple of years later, I participated in a VIA intensive online course, facilitated by Ryan Niemiec. He shared what successful strengths-based practitioners do to put character strengths into practice and presented the aware-explore-apply model.[181]

Aware

After the VIA Survey has been administered, the aware phase begins by examining the meaning of character strengths. Young people who have experienced adversity are very familiar with being labeled, though their experiences with labels largely are negative. Many carry a host of labels that identify what is wrong with them. Labeling is powerful and, over time, leads to a young person's becoming the label (e.g., I am depressed, bipolar, promiscuous, delinquent). However, when they suddenly learn that their top strengths are courage, forgiveness, creativity, leadership, and spirituality, they often are stunned. Steven and Sybil Wolin coined the term *survivor's pride*[182] to describe the positive and empowering reaction many youths have when people name their strengths.

During the aware phase, the youth practitioner supports the young person to understand the meaning of each of the character strengths. With adolescents, I often ask them to research their signature strengths by finding people in history, sports, or entertainments who embody those strengths and to summarize how the person used those strengths. Talking with young people about the ranking of their strengths and how the survey results fit their perceptions are good ways to raise awareness. Youth practitioners may use their dialogues to highlight that we have all character strengths and that lower strengths do not indicate deficits or weaknesses.

Youth practitioners can use strengths-spotting when they work with young people.[183] This requires that the practitioners have a good understanding of the twenty-four character strengths and that they are fully attuned to the young person. When people activate their signature strengths, they often use subtle verbal window-words or activate nonverbal windows. They may use other words to express kindness, such as generosity, caring, giving, or compassion, serving as windows to a signature strength. Nonverbal windows may include an expressive posture, hand movements, tone of voice, or smiling, or their "eyes may light up."[184] When youth practitioners notice verbal or nonverbal windows, they make affirmative statements. For example:

> Tatiana, I am touched by the way you can let go of the people who caused you pain. You affirm how important is to forgive people to move on with your life.

> Nick, I noticed how much credit you gave to your partner on the project you just presented. You are a real team player.

Explore

In the explore phase, the youth worker facilitates an exploration of the ways young people have used their strengths (particularly signature strengths) in their lives. To highlight strengths, the youth practitioner may begin by asking the young people to tell about times when they were at their best and then later may juxtapose this by asking what strengths they seem to use the least during times of excessive stress. Here is an example:

> Keith, aged fourteen, and his family moved into our neighborhood some years ago, and each day when I got home, he was outside. He often would come to my driveway and say, "Hi. How are you?" Within a couple of weeks, he was there every day to greet me, and we would talk for a bit. He was very observant of my every move, and one day, when my hands were full, he asked, "Should I check the mailbox for your?" He brought the mail to the front door and then said good-bye and left. Thereafter, he followed me to the door each day, and we often had long conversations on the front porch. He openly talked about the stress he experienced at home. His father was drinking, his mother was "depressed all the time," and his family was struggling to make ends meet with the income they had. I asked how he was able to deal with all these stressors in his life, and he answered, "I always find grown-ups I can talk with, like you. They support and encourage me, and I don't have

to think about what goes on at home at the time." As my relationship with Keith developed, I learned that he used his *love* signature strength to create a network of supportive adults at school and in the community.

The VIA Institute on Character has mapped character strengths on two dimensions, referred to as the two-factor balance graph: mind versus heart (self-regulation and perseverance vs. humor and gratitude) and interpersonal versus intrapersonal (humility and teamwork vs. love of learning and creativity).[185] During the exploration phase, the youth worker and young person may jointly color the young person's signature strengths on the map and then reflect on the balance. In the event a signature strength is not found in one or more of the quadrants, it possibly could be considered to explore and develop the use of one or more of the strengths from that quadrant to achieve balance.

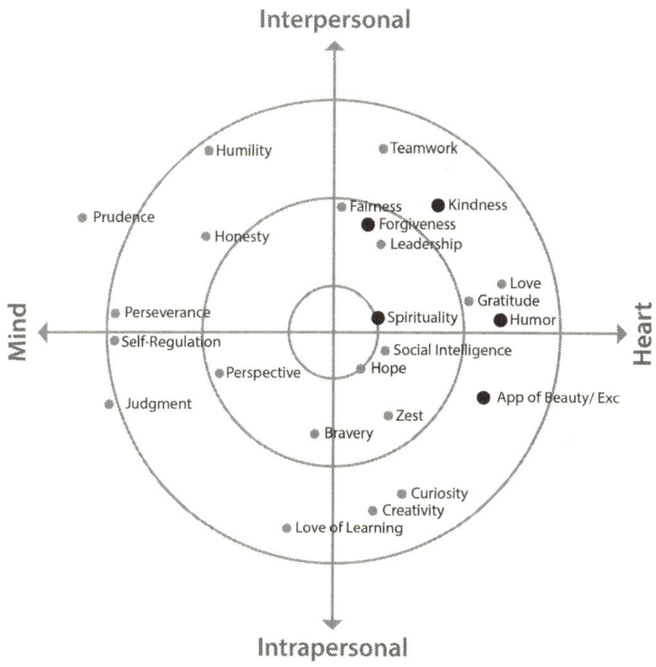

Figure 8. Character strengths mapping for Charissa Kline

Apply

In the apply phase, the youth practitioner helps young people to develop their strengths by asking which strength they want to work on. While a person can develop all strengths, signature strengths matter the most. A very practical way to start strengths development is to find a new way to use a signature strength each day. A young person with whom I worked decided to develop her perseverance strength and selected five ways to do it during the upcoming week: on day one she completed all her math problems without giving up. On day two she jogged one mile in PE class, and on the third day, she wrote an explanation of each of her signature strengths and discussed them with her English teacher, who generally was unable to see her positive sides. On the fourth day, she stayed awake and was engaged in science class (her least favorite class), and on the fifth day she practiced perseverance by listening and asking questions of her social studies project partner, rather than arguing.

You can also help young people develop their bottom strengths. Amanda, whose gratitude strength was ranked as number twenty-one, agreed to take ten minutes each day to meet with me and share what she was grateful for that day. For the first few days, it was hard for her to find anything she was grateful for, but after a couple of weeks, she began to change her view of her daily experiences and increased her ability to appreciate the positive events in her life.

A person can also develop an underused strength. Appreciation of beauty and excellence is one of my lowest strengths (number twenty). During a trip to Australia, I decided to increase my use of this strength by giving it special attention each day. On my daily walk, I brought my camera and focused on finding something I found beautiful—a flower, a bird, the skies, a house, a landscape, or a garden—and take a picture of it. I emailed the picture to my wife to share my experience. I have learned to increase my awareness of beauty, and I continue to bring it forward more frequently.

For more suggestions on developing character strengths, I recommend you use Rashid and Anjum's *340 Ways to use VIA Character Strengths.*[186]

Interconnection of Growth Needs and Character Strengths

The second intentional responsive adult practice—naming and developing young people's character strengths—help tip the scale toward positive outcomes. Character strengths are leveraged to support young people to meet their growth needs. Martin Seligman observed that people who use their character strengths each day pursue the good life and are on the path toward well-being and authentic happiness.[187]

Table 7. Growth needs and character strengths

Growth Needs	Character Strengths
Belonging	Social intelligence, love, kindness, humility, fairness, humor
Achievement	Creativity, curiosity, judgment, love of learning, perspective
Autonomy	Self-regulation, perseverance, prudence, judgment, leadership
Contribution	Kindness, forgiveness, zest, appreciation of beauty and excellence, humility, teamwork
Hope and purpose	Gratitude, hope, zest, spirituality, bravery

Character Strengths in Action

There are many ways to use character strengths with yourself and with young people. For example, McQuaid created a strengths mural in her son's bedroom, with pictures representing each of the character strengths.[188] That made it easy for her to talk with her son about strengths and to share stories about times when they or others used their strengths.

Character Strengths in Action

I Was at My Wit's End

Kasia Borkowski, a teacher in Western Australia, shared how she used character strengths with her students.[189]

> The students in my class (grades four through six) were constantly picking on each other. I was at my wit's end! I decided to teach them about character strengths and hoped it would help them see that all of them have something

positive to offer. I downloaded the character-strengths posters from the VIA website and laminated them to be ready for the kids the next day. I also created paper medal templates to be used in an activity.

I began the activity by asking my students to identify their three top strengths. Some students worked independently, and I helped others who were a bit timid or who did not exactly understand the names of the strengths. Looking back, it would have been helpful if I had worked with my assistant to explain the names of the strengths.

Next, I asked the students to make a poster titled "I Win a Medal for ..." (e.g., bravery) and to use the medal templates I had printed. I also asked them to list on the poster three other strengths that fit them. As they worked on their projects, I observed, encouraged, and guided them to choose a strength that fit them.

When the posters were done, we had a mat session. We talked about how everyone has all twenty-four character strengths and because we are different, we use some more often than others—and that's OK.

I have continued to point out when students use one of their strengths (e.g., kindness, bravery, compassion). It motivates them to look for positive characteristics in others, rather than picking on or bullying them. If the picking begins, I ask them to stop and identify a strength instead.

The activity increased my confidence. I have continued to point out their strengths, and they are beginning to see different sides of each other. Some of the kids also have started to point out their peers' strengths. That creates quite a supportive environment.

Healing with Character Strengths

Wade Puryear, vice president of education at a school in Virginia that serves students with special education needs, shared how the school uses character strengths to help their students bounce back from adversity.[190]

> We serve students between ages seven and twenty-one. All of them complete the VIA Survey at admission, the younger students with help from adults. Within the next couple of weeks, the students, along with their coaches, explore the results of their VIA reports. They discuss if the signature strengths fit the students' ideas about themselves. When students learn that their strengths have names, and they can talk with others about them, they get excited. Some of the strengths names are very familiar to the students, while others are new. That gives us a chance to learn the meaning of a new word. It is like learning a foreign language. We stick to the VIA strengths names because it is easier to talk about strengths when we use the same language. It also makes it easier to ask students to do strengths-spotting with their peers.
>
> The students and the coaches explore how their signature strengths influence thoughts, emotions, motivations, and behavior. After we have explored the students' signature strengths, we talk about how strong their other character strengths are. We have all twenty-four strengths; some, the signature strengths, are simply those that are most used and visible to us and others across different contexts. Our coaches meet weekly with the students to plan how they can develop and use their strengths.

Staff in many schools and residential centers, as well as caregivers, support young people as they develop their strengths. In some schools, character strengths are used to develop goals. Following are examples that illustrate the integration of character strengths and growth goals into objectives for several young people.

1. Jasmine will use her love strength for her family by posting pictures and quotes of herself on Instagram (belonging).
2. Paul will use his zest and creativity strengths to create three-minute brain breaks for his classmates and will, at his teacher's request, lead one activity daily (achievement).
3. With the support of the assistant teacher, Zoe will develop her prudence strength to review risks and advantages of leisure activities. She will use an iPad to design posters for the classroom (autonomy).
4. Javar will increase his self-control strength by independently using the Stop, Breathe, & Think app on his iPad, with 80 percent success in four out of five stressful situations (autonomy).
5. Nikita will increase her bravery strength to increase her kindness strength by volunteering at the outdoor challenge camp for two weeks this summer (contributing).
6. Rich will increase his hope strength by taking pictures of places, people, and ideas that represent his hope for the future. He and his youth worker will use their scheduled outings to capture the pictures over a two-week period. Rich will then select one picture that best shows his hope for the future. He will then write an essay and make a YouTube video about his hope (hope and purpose).

Reflections

- Develop a plan to use one of your signature strengths each day for a week. Then pick another for the following week.
- Pick one of your character strengths that you would like to develop. Practice it each day, and share your experience with another person.
- Sign up for the VIA Character Strengths blog at http://www.viacharacter.org/blog/
- Go strengths-spotting. For ideas, see http://www.viacharacter.org/blog/?s=strengths+spotting.

Explorations

- Watch Ryan M. Niemiec's TEDx talk, "A Universal Language That Describes What's Best in Us."[191]
- Read *Character Strengths Interventions* by Ryan M. Niemiec.[192]
- Read *Mindfulness and Character Strengths: A Practical Guide to Flourishing* by Ryan M. Niemiec.[193]
- Read *Character Strengths Matter. How to Live a Full Life* by Shannon Polly and Kathryn Britton.[194]

9

Solidifying Executive Functions

To be successful in life and in relationships, people must learn to self-regulate, solve problems, organize, remember information, learn from mistakes, manage impulses, and focus their attention. These abilities are known as executive functions and self-regulation skills. They involve three broad types of brain functioning: inhibitory control, working memory, and mental flexibility.[195] One of these executive functions, working memory, has been shown to be a stronger predictor than IQ of success in reading, spelling, and math.[196]

Children who live with chronic, unpredictable stress have few opportunities to develop strong executive functions because they use their brain capacity to head off or cope with the next traumatic event. These young people can benefit greatly from safe environments with caring adults who understand that youth cope the best they can. With this mind-set, youth practitioners intentionally can engage young people in experiences that build their executive functions. When a young person struggles with impulse control, youth practitioners must use their knowledge about the brain to remind themselves that the child did not just decide to be uncaring or reckless. What others may think is a minor challenge or a small disappointment may flood children's brains with stress hormones that prevent them from inhibiting their impulses and predicting the consequences of their behaviors. The best emotional first aid in situations like this may be to encourage young people to take deep breaths to slow down their heart rates, which brings more oxygen to the brain and lowers blood pressure.

Understanding Executive Functions

Genetics, gender, family environment, life experiences, nutrition, and stress, among other factors, influence the development of executive functions. Parents and practitioners can do many things to help young people exercise executive functions. When adults know about a child's stage of brain development, they can provide the right amount of support and modeling. If, instead of support, punishment is used, adults can stifle the development of executive functions.

The foundation of executive functions is laid down in the brain early in life through serve-and-return interactions. Because the brain is malleable, executive functions continue to develop throughout childhood and adolescence in the context of supportive adults and ecologies.[197] The development of inhibitory control and working memory shows dramatic development early in life. Toddlers develop independence by learning to override automatic responses, also known as inhibition or self-regulation. They also develop working memory that allows them to hold information long enough to process the information needed to complete tasks. Around age five, children develop foundational skills in mental flexibility, used to plan, attend, and organize. Over the next twenty years of life, these brain systems become increasingly integrated, faster, and more sophisticated.

Inhibitory control, or impulse control, is the capacity to scrutinize distractions, stay focused, override impulses, resist temptation, think before acting, and persist in the face of worry or adversity. Inhibitory control helps children wait until called upon and take turns in interactions with others. Impulse control, also often called self-regulation, stops people from yelling or hitting other people when they get frustrated.

Working memory is the capacity to access, hold, and manage information over short periods of time (typically one to twenty minutes) to stay with and complete a task or activity. It gives people the ability to think of multiple things at the same time and to hone in on something while keeping something else in the back of the mind. Working memory allows people to smoothly pick up an activity or task after an interruption and to follow complex instructions (e.g., "Your paper must be five pages not including the cover page and references, typed double-space with a twelve-point font size, and then uploaded online by 6:00 p.m. on May 12." In school and life, working memory helps people link information from one source to another, such as remembering the steps in converting fractions into percentages.

Mental or cognitive flexibility is the ability to easily shift between modes of thinking and to simultaneously consider multiple ideas or perceptions. It helps people revise their beliefs, adapt to changes, adjust plans, revamp priorities, learn from failure, be creative, and use different rules or social skills in different settings.

In summary, executive functions and self-regulation involve a collection of processes responsible for cognitive, emotional, and behavioral functions in multiple situations and contexts. These interrelated functions allow people to focus attention, manage emotions, remember instructions, plan, and regulate their responses. Executive functions have been called the brain's "air traffic control system."

Executive Functions in Action

Young people develop executive functioning skills beginning early in life and continuing throughout childhood and adolescence, stimulated by healthy interactions with parents and other adults in their environment.

Experiences and Games to Exercise Executive Functions

Executive functions can be exercised throughout life. Caregivers and youth practitioners can engage young people in activities that develop executive functions in natural settings. The Center on the Developing Child at Harvard University provides a guide with games and activities that support the development of executive functions from infancy to adolescence.[198] From early childhood through young adulthood, card games, board games, physical games, dance, and drama are fun and meaningful ways to help children exercise their executive functions. Almost all card games require the participants to pay attention and follow rules and offer the opportunity to exercise working memory, while still others stretch cognitive flexibility.

Strengthening Executive Functions through Project-Based Learning

Craig Simmons, a licensed professional counselor in Virginia, shared how he supports students in strengthening their executive functions at the school where he works.[199]

> Our school serves students with neurological differences and students with long stories of adverse life events. Since almost all of them struggle with executive functions (EF), we decided to find ways to help them strengthen their EF skills. To be intentional about that, we decided to use the Behavior Rating Inventory of Executive Function (BRIEF) at intake and have both the student and a parent complete the assessment.[200]
>
> We share and explore the results of the BRIEF with the student and parent in a joint meeting—both strong and weak areas and areas where the student and the parent rated EF skills differently. The BRIEF explores ten domains of executive functions, as shown in Table 8.
>
> A couple of days ago, I met with sixteen-year-old Ophelia and her mother to talk about her results on the BRIEF. Ophelia and her mom both rated working memory and organize materials as stronger areas. Since Ophelia came to the school, her teachers have observed that she often stuffs her emotions until she either erupts or implodes. The BRIEF showed that Ophelia perceived her inhibit and emotional control as low, while her mother rated them as average. Ophelia's mom was surprised to learn that her daughter was struggling in this area. During the meeting, the three of us developed ways for Mom to become more tuned in and supportive of Ophelia's emotions to prevent meltdowns. Ophelia was relieved that

her mother understood her better and suggested that she herself begin to ask Mom and others for support when she feels swamped by her emotions.

Table 8. Executive functioning and self-regulation abilities[201]

		Ability
Behavior regulation	Inhibit	Resist impulses, and think about the consequences of action before acting.
	Self-monitor	Have awareness of the effect of one's own behavior and how it impacts others.
Emotional regulation	Shift	Transition smoothly, tolerate change, problem-solve flexibly, and switch attention from one focus or topic to another.
	Emotional control	Have ability to express and regulate one's emotions.
Metacognition	Initiate	Have ability to generate ideas and responses, and problem-solve.
	Task completion	Complete school work or chores in a timely fashion; finish tests within time limits; work at satisfactory pace.
	Working memory	Hold information in mind to complete a task; encode and store information; or generate goals.
	Plan and organize	Anticipate future events; set goals; develop appropriate steps ahead of time to carry out an associated task or action; carry out tasks in a systematic manner; understand and communicate main ideas or key concepts.
	Task monitor	Check work; evaluate performance during or shortly after finishing a task to ensure expected completion.
	Organize materials	Organize things in one's environment, including work, play, and storage spaces (e.g., school desks, lockers, backpacks, and bedrooms).

The BRIEF also has shown that many of our students struggle with working memory and planning and organization. Through practice, we have learned that the best way to help students exercise these EF areas is through project-based learning. For example, Zach, one of our students with neurological differences, is really struggling in both areas. He has attended the school for two years and is now motivated to improve his EF skills. During one of my meetings with Zach, we developed a project where he could work on his EF skills. We decided that he would plan and emcee a lip-sync "battle" at the school. With the support of staff and a peer, Zach planned every detail, from recruiting lip-sync participants to developing promotional flyers, reserving the venue and AV equipment, and emceeing the battle. He worked tirelessly to develop detailed written plans to organize the day and exercised his working memory by remembering the details he needed as the emcee. The battle was a great success, and Zach had the best EF exercises of his life.

The project also offered an opportunity for Zach's partner, Jake, to exercise and strengthen his inhibit and emotional control. Jake is also neurologically different and obsesses on AV equipment and getting the sound perfect. However, when things don't go his way, he easily flips his lid and starts throwing things around. I was quite concerned to make him responsible for the expensive equipment and talked with him about it. He assured me that, if given this responsibility, he would "control" himself. During the month of preparation, Jake repeatedly sought advice on understanding his triggers and how to calm himself. He learned and practiced deep breathing and mindfulness exercises on a daily basis to calm himself. The event was a big success for him too.

Reflections

- Identify one thing you can do to strengthen executive functions in young people.
- Reflect on your own executive functions. Then assess one of your skills at http://www.psytoolkit.org/experiment-library/nback.html or https://www.youtube.com/watch?v=j1Amj5JydXU

Explorations

- *Enhancing and Practicing Executive Function Skills with Children from Infancy to Adolescence* from the Center on the Developing Child at Harvard University.[202]
- Read *FLIPP the Switch: Strengthen Executive Function Skills* by Sheri Wilkins and Carol Burmeister.[203]

10

Tapping into Culture and Spirituality

> If we open-mindedly examine how people live, we can move beyond using ethnic labels that assign predetermined characteristics to people. We can think of culture as communities' ways of living. Our focus thus becomes people's participation in cultural practices. This helps us understand the commonalities and differences that exist both within and among cultural communities ... and communities' changes and continuities.[204]
>
> —Barbara Rogoff

Young people thrive when they use their character strengths, draw on their executive functions, have strong supportive relationships with adults and positive peers, are strongly grounded in their culture, and affirm their faith. Research on risk and resilience shows that cultural participation provides the foundation for stability (meaning, history, continuity, and identity) and hope (faith and future orientation) in people's lives.[205]

We think of culture as people's and communities' ways of living, expressed through beliefs, customs, art, traditions, and rituals. Zaretta Hammond compared culture to a tree and the ecosystem that surrounds it.[206] The tree, with its roots, trunk, branches, bark, leaves, and fruits, grows in constant interchange with the ecosystem around it. Culture, just like the tree, has many "layers." People participate at three cultural levels: surface, shallow, and deep. The surface and shallow cultures are constantly changing as people meet and interact with one another, influenced by the ecosystem around them. Deep culture, on the other hand, anchors individuals and nourishes their psychosocial growth. Just like the roots keep the tree secured, deep culture anchors the way people understand and relate to the world. Often referred to as their worldview or belief system, it is the foundation of self-concept, group identity, problem-solving approaches, and decision making. Over time, deep culture leads to the development of a mental map that determines how people interpret reality and what they believe to be true. It influences values and faith and gives meaning to people as individuals and as members of families, communities, tribes, and nations.

Deep culture is intertwined in the ecologies where children and youth interact. Barbara Rogoff explains that "culture is often treated as a set of ethnic 'boxes'—such as Latino, African American, Asian—that individuals 'belong in.' And they can belong in only one box. All people 'in' an ethnic box are assumed to be alike in an enduring and essentially in-born fashion."[207] This is a deficit approach to understanding culture, and it stereotypes people of like ethnic backgrounds to hold the same beliefs and behaviors. I do not hold this belief and understand culture as constantly changing and evolving within and across communities and generations.

Spectrum of Cultural Practices

Youth practitioners need a way to detect and learn about different cultural practices to help young people feel comfortable and safe. Table 8 highlights differences in cultural practices described as two extremes.[208] Neither is good nor bad; they are just opposites.

Table 9. Spectrum of cultural practices[209]

Individual Orientation	Group Orientation
Act individually	Act cooperatively
Individual decisions	Group decisions
Nonconformist	Conforming to social norms
Individuals before team	Team before individuals

Equality	Hierarchy
Self-directed	Leader directed
Individual initiative	Leader controlled
Flexible roles and expectations	Firm roles and expectations
Freedom to challenge	Do not challenge authority
Offer own opinion	Respect status of leaders

Direct Communication	Indirect Communication
Focus is on what is said, not how it is said	Focus on how it is said
Engage in conflict	Avoid conflict
Short, direct questions	Importance of being friendly
Focus on information	Focus on feeling
Express opinions directly	Express opinions diplomatically

Task Orientation	Relationship Orientation
Focus on time-keeping	Focus on relationship building
Goal: Provide accurate information	Goal: Create a feel-good atmosphere
Define people by what they do	Define people by who they know
Logic orientation	Feeling orientation

Guilt	Shame
Responsible for individual sin	Responsible for corporate sin
Results from individual action	Results from identity
You made a mistake	You are a mistake
Absolved by confession	Absolved by status change

Of course, no one group of people's cultural practices fall completely at either end of the spectrum; rather, cultural practices reflect a mixture. The spectrum represents two extremes of people's cultural practices and can help youth practitioners become culturally competent, beginning with an awareness of their own cultural practices.

Cultural incompetence is characterized by cultural blindness or cultural bias. Cultural blindness is shown when a person is unaware of or cannot describe his or her own cultural preferences. Cultural bias is expressed when a person or organization believes that there is one best way to relate to one another. Cultural bias often results in the minority group having to change its behaviors to fit in with the dominant group. When this is the case in youth-adult interactions, the young person cannot feel safe with the youth practitioner.

Cultural Dimensions

Geert Hofstede, one of the first sociologists to examine the effects of culture on people's values and beliefs, identified six dimensions in national cultures.[210] These six dimensions are described in appendix C. While youth practitioners focus on understanding how cultural practices shape deep brain development in young people, Hofstede's dimensions provide another framework to explore cultural practices.

Based on extensive data-gathering and analysis from more than seventy countries, Hofstede and his team generated an index of national cultures.[211] For example—and not surprisingly—the United States has the highest individualism score of all countries in the data set. This means that culture practices expressed in government institutions and organizations tend to reflect an individualistic orientation. However, many adults and young people participate in cultural practices in their homes and communities that may reflect collectivistic approaches. Most schools and youth organizations in the United States, Canada, New Zealand, Australia, and other areas that were colonized by Europeans tend to reflect individualistic practices.

When children are met with cultural practices that are incongruent with their deep culture, internal dissonance and psychosocial pain can block their ability to learn and feel safe. At worst, imposition of a dominant belief system through coercion is abusive and traumatic, resulting in significant pain.

Dominator Cultures

Throughout history, dominator cultures have suppressed cultural practices and destroyed the language, values, and traditions of minority groups.

The history of slavery and discrimination in the United States is one such example. In South Africa, the apartheid system methodically destroyed the population's traditions and ways of life. For almost a century, the governments of Australia, Canada, and the United States systematically removed indigenous children as young as six years old from their parents and placed them in residential schools. The schools were located far away from the children's communities, making it difficult—often impossible—for children to be with their families. In these schools, jointly operated by churches and governments, children were not allowed to speak their native language, wear their traditional clothes, or practice their cultural beliefs.

Through these policies, as well as individual and organizational actions, strong attempts were made to rip away indigenous belief systems and force compliance to the beliefs and cultural traditions of the dominant society. Thousands of children and families were traumatized and now live painfully and courageously with the intergenerational wounds that remain.

Cultural Competence

Cultural explorations often focus on the different ways people participate in a culture. Nevertheless, there are many similarities among all cultures.[212] People in all cultures

- face birth, life, and death;
- are concerned with survival;
- are concerned with interpreting the universe;
- have rules structuring social relationships;
- use language to transmit cultural practices from one generation to the next; and
- are concerned with perpetuating their cultural practices.

When adults respect a young person's deep brain cultural values, the young person feels safe and can be open to experiences and advice that promote growth and development. Similarly, in multicultural environments, young people can use cultural practices to develop resilience and meet their need for belongingness.

Youth practitioners are encouraged to become culturally responsive by learning to recognize their own deep brain culture and become curious and open-minded to young people who bring different cultural practices.

Culture and Faith in Action

First Nations, Metis, and Inuit Courses Saved My Life

Tricia Giles-Wang, a health and well-being consultant with First Nations, Metis, and Inuit Education in Alberta, Canada, shared the following story:[213]

> Adam, a grade-eleven student, has struggled with being hopeful and finding purpose for several years and at times has had suicidal ideations. Earlier this year, he signed up to participate in a one-credit bow-hunting weekend course offered to First Nations, Metis, and Inuit students.
>
> Adam became very engaged during the course and enjoyed the teachings from the teacher, an elder. He also connected with other indigenous students. While using a hatchet to carve out his bow, Adam thanked the teacher for offering traditional indigenous-based courses to First Nations, Metis, and Inuit students. Adam disclosed to the teacher that he had been diagnosed with depression for a few years and talked about his ups and downs, as well as suicidal ideations. Very emotionally, Adam said, "I get to reconnect with my culture and spirituality by participating in indigenous courses like this. The courses and lacrosse have saved my life." He also shared that his father, who is First Nations, has completely assimilated into postcolonial society and encourages him not to pursue his culture. His mother, also First Nations, on the other hand, has walked alongside Adam's journey to reconnect with his culture and identity.

> Approximately a week after the bow-hunting course, Adam's school contacted the teacher. Adam was in a very bad low. Since he had spoken so positively about the bow-hunting course, the school asked if the elder would come to meet with him. The elder agreed and met Adam at the school and gifted him with a smudge kit. During their time together, the elder suggested that Adam become a leader and bring cultural opportunities to his peers at his school by leading a weekly smudge. Adam was a little hesitant and wanted some time to think about it. A few weeks later, the teacher learned that Adam had led his first smudge at the school. It lifted his spirits and gave him such a sense of pride and purpose.
>
> Adam continues to lead a weekly smudge at his high school. He still struggles with ups and downs but now has a stronger sense of identity because he can turn to his culture and spirituality to guide him through those tough times.

Reclaiming My South Sudanese Name and Culture

Gregg Morris, lead educator and creator at Mahana Culture in Victoria, Australia, shared how learning and participation in cultural practices empowered a young man.[214]

> Bakhit and his family came to Australia as refugees from South Sudan around 2000. I met him through a church friend about ten years later and got to know him when he entered a youth-worker certificate program, where I was a facilitator. The program is a two-year journey in which students develop skills in community development and in working with young people from different cultures. Therefore, an important part of the program is learning to understand and use culture in youth work. Students learn about Maori traditions, dances, and speaking the

language. During their two-year study, students explore in depth how indigenous cultures systematically were destroyed by Western imperialism in many parts of the world and then were followed by racism.

Bakhit was surprised to learn about the emphasis we placed on culture and shared the humiliation and ridicule he experienced when he first came to Australia. In school, teachers did not try to learn to pronounce his name. When they attempted to pronounce his name, other students would laugh. He felt like an outsider and decided to go by the name Shaggy, after his favorite rap singer, and never to speak his native language, Dinka, again.

Towards the end of Shaggy's program, I took the group to New Zealand to visit and learn from different communities. We visited a contemporary monastery that welcomes people who struggle, people who seek prayerful retreat, and those who seek a missional lifestyle. During our visit, we had a *hāngi*, a traditional Maori method of cooking food on heated rocks buried in a pit. Our youth workers were astonished with the ease and respect with which our hosts, a group of white guys, spoke Maori and followed traditional ways of coking, welcoming people, and much more. As we were ready to begin the meal, Shaggy was asked to say a prayer. He began speaking in a language I had never heard him use before—Dinka—and then continued in Arabic. The experience at the monastery gave him the power to reclaim Dinka, his name (Bakhit), and culture. It helped him rediscover himself and what he stands for in this world.

After the completion of the program, he was recruited to work as a multicultural development officer at a football club. He supported young migrants and refugees and their communities in learning the Australian ways of doing things while remaining proud of their indigenous cultures.

Following a clash between a mostly South Sudanese gang and a Pacific Islander gang in Australia, many of the suspected leaders were arrested and sent to prison. Shaggy quit his job at the football club and now works in the prison to help reconcile the two groups.

Reflections

- Reflect on your own cultural practices at the deep, shallow, and surface levels.
- What beliefs and assumptions shape your deep culture?
- What questions would you ask to learn about the cultural practices of a young person?
- What actions could you take to assist a young person who requires spiritual or religious support?

Explorations

- Read *Culturally Responsive Teaching and the Brain: Promoting Authentic Engagement and Rigor among Culturally and Linguistic Diverse Students* by Zaretta Hammond.[215]
- Read *Many Colors: Cultural Intelligence for a Changing Church* by Soong-Chan Rah.[216]

11

Intentional Solution-Finding Practices

In previous chapters, we looked at the impact that nurture and stress have on young people's growth and development. The psychosocial and intellectual development is disrupted for many children who live with abuse, neglect, or other adverse experiences. When adults, whether caregivers or youth practitioners, learn to respond with care and support to children in pain, rather than reacting, they can help tip the scale toward positive outcomes. Fortunately, positive outcomes help young people meet the five universal growth needs:

- Belonging in an ecology of relatedness
- Achievement of goals and coping with challenges
- Autonomy to regulate emotions and actions
- Contribution to others and the community
- Hope and purpose

Beyond awareness and knowledge about brain development, toxic stress, relationships, character strengths, executive functions, and culture, youth practitioners need solution-focused practices to help struggling young people develop resilience. In the following, I will describe six responsive practices which are illustrated in Figure 9.

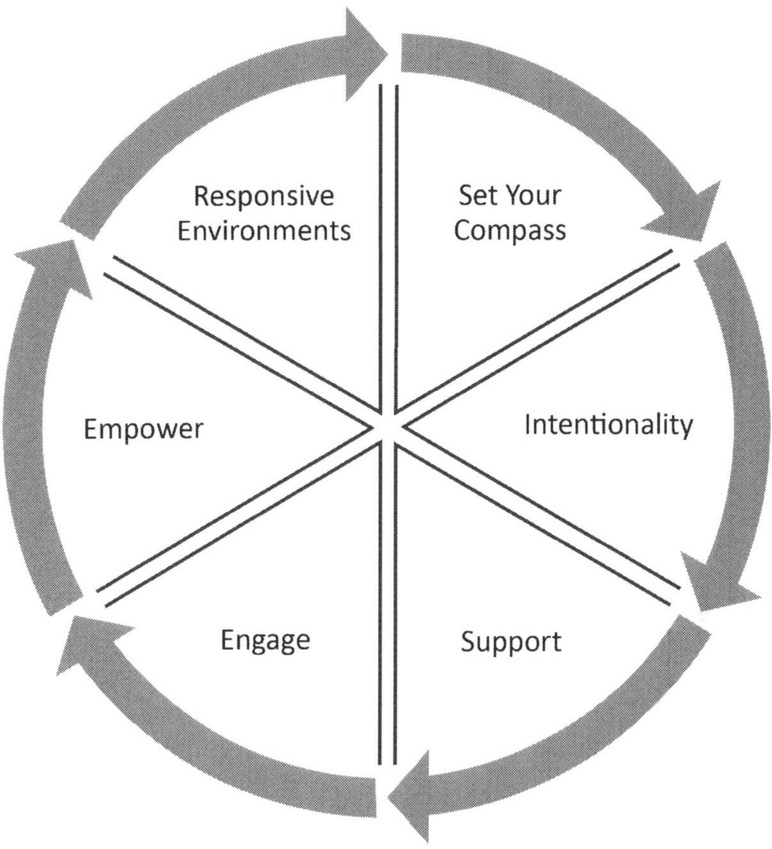

Figure 9. Intentional solution-finding practices

The solution-finding practices are not sequential steps, nor do they all need to be completed at a given time. They form a continuum and can be used in any format that makes sense with a young person or a group of young people. In the here and now, they can be used as crisis intervention, behavior support, or as a brief interaction to support a positive outcome. Short-term usage may span from twenty-four hours to a week, where a youth practitioner uses the practices in a series of classes or counseling sessions or during a weekend camping trip. Long-term use of responsive practices can be used to support a youth during a sports season, while in foster care or a residential program, or over the course of a school year.

Young people can learn to use solution-focused practices to support friends and relatives. I encourage you to teach young people the practices and processes.

Practice 1—Set Your Compass

Raising strong and resilient young people involves parenting and discipline practices represented by two different paradigms: the authoritarian (coercive) and the responsive (collaborative) paradigms.

Paradigms reflect our beliefs and guide how we view and interact with young people, whether we are parents or youth practitioners. Paradigms are ingrained into the deep brain and are passed on from generation to generation. They do not change easily. Both research and practice wisdom demonstrate that the responsive paradigm excels in supporting all young people to achieve positive outcomes, particularly for children who have experienced toxic stress.

Table 10. Authoritarian and responsive paradigms

Authoritarian	Responsive
Relationships of trust and respect are secondary, or unimportant, and one-sided. Power imbalance between adult and young person.	Relationships are primary and characterized by trust, cooperation, and mutual respect. Balanced power between adult and young person.
Coercive and controlling, adultism. Reward and punishment. Willingness to manipulate and exclude young people.	Authoritative. In control of self and the situation without controlling youth. Consistent willingness to engage and include.
Use pain to deal with pain-based behavior.	Use knowledge, skills, and relationship to deal with pain-based behavior.
Focus on compliance and fixing behavior.	Focus on teaching and growth.
Regulation from outside, fostering dependency.	Regulation from inside, fostering self-regulation and self-efficacy.
Enforcement of rules; inflexible. Dominated by blanket rules. "I said so"; "Because that's the rule."	Teaching and guiding with high expectations regarding values and principles. Clear routines and boundaries with few necessary rules.
Adults react to the outside kid – behavior.	Adults respond to the inside kid – the deep brain.
Deficit focus—"What's going wrong?" Seek to fix young people.	Strength focus—"What's going right?" Seek to meet growth needs.

Though no person operates exclusively from one of these paradigms, particularly in challenging situations, most adults act according to one or the other. I invite and encourage you to strengthen your responsive paradigm by using what you have learned about growth and development, the intentional responsive adult practices, and the six problem-solving practices we are about to explore. Though some of this may be awkward at first, remember that your brain is malleable. By practicing new ways of responding to young people in pain, you will develop strong neural connections to support young people on their life journeys.

Practice 2—Intentionality

> To create healing presence, we fine-tune our inner experience to the inner state of the other person. We transform ourselves in response to the basic needs of the person we are trying to heal and to help. Ultimately, we find within ourselves the psychological and spiritual resources required to nourish and to empower the other human being.[217]
>
> —Peter Breggin

Responding to pain with care is a natural ability. When people see someone in distress, their instinct is to help, unless there is an immediate threat to their own safety or that of others. History is filled with examples of human courage and compassion. It is that instinct we draw upon in interactions with young people. Adults can learn to recognize psychosocial pain and respond compassionately. Caring responses from others free the youth to explore their actions and make positive choices in the future. Nurturance and understanding prevent young people from getting stuck in pain-based cycles that interfere with meeting growth needs.

Young people who have lived with abusive, neglectful, and unpredictable adults are often reluctant to connect and relate to adults. To reach these young people, youth practitioners must be intentional. Intentionality involves tuning in to one's own thoughts and emotions to become fully present, relating to and understanding the young person.

Intentional adults use natural events to reach out and engage everything they know about young people and their histories, character strengths, executive functions, culture, and faith. It includes listening, giving a glance of acknowledgement or support or a pat on the back, or simply being with the young person. Intentionality activates the social synapse connecting the young person and the adult at a deep-brain level. In summary, intentional adults think, relate, and understand—they are TRU.

Think

When a young person experiences high levels of stress, youth practitioners can reestablish a sense of calm by tapping into their own deep brain. When they manage their own feelings, they can mobilize executive functions, culture, and strengths to calm the young person. Following an amygdala hijack, stress hormones can stay in the body for up to twenty-four hours.

In emotionally charged situations, the thinking brain can cue a person to realize that he or she currently is adding stress to the situation and needs to change course. With this self-awareness, the youth practitioner can override alarm signals from the amygdala and become fully present to evaluate and respond to the situation. In this state of mindfulness, the adult can be intentional about his or her responses. Intentional adults think before they act and use their thinking brains to become self-aware and fully present. With this mind-set, they can engage their own strengths to respond to the situation.

Tit for Tat

Without becoming mindful, people are likely to respond with friendliness when met with friendliness and with hostility when met with hostility. This is called "tit for tat," which means that people often respond to an action in the way it was given to them. Tit-for-tat responses are common and are considered to be the most appropriate approach to use in interpersonal communication. Recent research has identified other strategies that are equally or more successful than tit for tat.[218] For example, ignoring aggression and responding in a friendly and supportive manner produces equal or better outcomes. Therefore, tit for tat is a poor strategy for parenting, teaching, and helping young people cope with stress because it often results in a vicious cycle of fighting pain with pain.

Relate

> Every child needs at least one adult who is irrationally crazy about him or her.[219]
>
> —Urie Bronfenbrenner

> Stability means finding people who regulate you well and staying near them.[220]
>
> —Thomas Lewis, Richard Amini, and Fari Lannon

Children are born to bond with close caregivers, and their "brains are wired to develop in tandem with another's, through emotional communication, beginning before words are spoken. If these things go awry, you're going to have seeds of psychological problems, of difficulty coping, stress in human relations, substance abuse, those sorts of problems later on."[221] Making up for adverse experiences requires a lot of energy, if not heroic interventions later in life.

The human brain is wired for life in community with others to protect the group, including the weakest and most vulnerable members. Darwin's notion of survival of the fittest may induce images of strong, muscular, guarded, and aggressive people, though in real life, "those who are nurtured best, survive best."[222] Our capacity for empathy and self-regulation is shaped by the experiences people have with others in their ecology, beginning early in life.[223]

The strongest protective factor for children and youth is the caring relationship with a positive adult. Such relationships assist the brain in developing secure attachments and regulate affect arousal. In the absence of caring adults, the brain's circuitry develops loose connections, resulting in poor coping skills. In the absence of caring adults, young people may meet their need for belonging through relationships with peers who often fall short of providing them with what they seek.[224] Caring relationships are associated with better physical health, while impoverished relationships often increase stress-hormone levels and lower immune functioning. The evidence is overwhelming—youth thrive in places with an abundance of caring relationships. Relationships are the glue that keeps cultures together, whether in families, schools, youth organizations, or communities.[225]

The amygdala constantly scans the environment to determine if the social setting and people in it are safe. This unconscious safety-threat detection system is called neuroception and immediately lets young people know if a person trying to connect with them is safe.[226] Since youth practitioners spend large amounts of time with young people, they are often the first responders when kids become overwhelmed by stress in schools, the community, or residential centers. First responders who show warmth, respect, compassion, and trust can help young people reestablish safety and calm. This matters to young people, in the moment and over time, because they want to know that adults in their lives care enough to understand them in their best and worst moments. In their worst moments, they need to feel safe and respected and that they count.

The Inside Kid

Intentional adults know that behaviors are outside expressions of what goes on deep inside the brain. They observe, listen, and ask questions to understand the inside kid.[227] With curiosity, these adults seek to understand the young person's experiences, culture, relationships, character strengths, and executive functions and his or her ability to engage these in challenging situations.

When youth practitioners ignore the inside kid and attempt to change young people from the outside, they do not support the development of resilience in young people. Adults need to go deep to explore the world of the inside kid—that unique combination of culture, the ways they meet their growth needs, and the meaning they attach to their experiences. Mark Freado and his colleague describe in detail the strategies for reaching the inside kid.[228]

Understand

Listening and understanding may not require words. In instances of deep angst, the most important—and respectful—response is deeply attentive and quiet listening. This shows that the adult is fully present, and it invites young people to tell their stories and express emotions without interruption. Intentional adults listen for the emotions and thoughts to understand the inside kid. This interest in the young person does not mean that the adult accepts the young person's behavior. Supportive adults do not allow or excuse hurting and hurtful behaviors to persist.

Chronic adverse events are not isolated occurrences, and young people cope the best they can in the moment. Due to intense stress, they often develop behavioral patterns in which they become stuck.

Verbal and Nonverbal Windows

Window words are words or phrases that give an opportunity to inquire further to understand a young person's worldview—a window to the inside kid. For example, a youth practitioner talks with a young person who has just thrown a chair across the room and hears the young person yell, "You're just like my mom!" This is a window phrase, which the youth practitioner later can explore: "You said I am just like your mom, what did you mean by that? I'd like to understand."

A young person also may respond with body language to questions or comments during a conversation. For example, a girl who had been bullied by her peers became tearful when her teacher affirmingly said, "You don't deserve to be treated like that." We call this a nonverbal window.

Practice 3—Support

Support is unconditional and is a core adult response ability; the young person does not have to earn it. Youth practitioners support young people because they understand their vulnerabilities in crisis situations and the impact of living with unpredictable chronic stress. When young people experience an amygdala hijack, their brains are flooded by stress hormones.

They need support to reengage their thinking brains. Through coregulation, a supportive adult can help young people regulate their emotions and draw on their strengths and executive functions to turn toxic stress into tolerable stress. Coregulation is the ability to utilize relationships to either stimulate or calm, keeping oneself inside the zone of tolerance.[229]

Young people who grow up with nurturing and support learn to self-regulate through scaffolding and role modeling. They can calm themselves when arousal rises to the limit of their tolerance levels, or they can stimulate themselves when arousal drops to their lower limits.

When adults are unaware of the consequences of toxic stress, they may themselves be in a heightened emotional state and resort to coercive regulation to appear to be in control. Coercion is a form of rankism—in this case, adultism—characterized by an aggressive tone of voice and retaliation, while ignoring a child's needs. Rankism describes situations where a person in a power position takes himself or herself to be "a somebody" and uses coercion to control people he or she considers "a nobody."[230]

Children and youth learn best from an adult with whom they have a strong, positive relationship. A practitioner who is not trusted or who does not know the young person well may not have a calming effect. In such situations, the adult should connect the young person with someone else in his or her ecology to with whom he or she is close (e.g., another teacher, youth worker, an elder, or a parent). Young people tend to choose the adults to whom they relate, and youth practitioners should not take these choices personally.

Safety

The brain's safety detection system is turned on twenty-four/seven because safety is fundamental to relatedness and well-being. When the need for safety is met, children and youth can focus attention on more complex developmental tasks vital to their growth. To ensure safety, the social and psychological environment must be free from physical and psychological harm. If a threat is detected, the brain shuts down executive functions and commits its entire bandwidth to dealing with the unsafe conditions. When young people do not feel safe, they cannot connect. Felt safety means that young people know they will not be harmed; rather, they are seen and soothed.

We will explore four domains of safety, each of them important and each interacting and overlapping with the others. These domains are physical, cultural, emotional, and social safety. Without felt safety in all four domains, young people cannot learn to trust people or their environment.

Physical Safety

When the adults in a school, youth program, or residential treatment center protect young people from physical harm, the young people feel psychologically and physically safe. Psychological safety is experienced when the adults enforce policies and practices that protect young people from sexual, racial, gender, and other forms of harassment. Organizations that offer peer mediation and other restorative practices to resolve conflicts and broken relationships enhance the feeling of safety for young people. Young people and adults feel physically secure when they are protected from violence, theft, exposure to weapons and threats, etc. While physical safety involves security measures, such as door locks, metal detectors, evacuation plans, emergency preparedness, and safe buildings and equipment, the sense of safety is experienced when adults consistently respond to unsafe situations.

Cultural Safety

Cultural safety focuses on the experiences of young people when they participate in an ecology with a different culture than their own.[231] They feel safe when they are encouraged to express their culture and spirituality without having to explain or being judged. Culturally competent youth workers are fully aware of their own culture and have the capacity to support the young person's development by integrating multiple cultural practices into the ecology. In this context, the young person feels comfortable and safe because different values and beliefs are recognized and respected, and a dominant culture is not forced on them. They are not expected to give up their cultural heritage to "fit in." Instead, they are nurtured as unique human beings with their dignity safeguarded. Young people are not coerced into taking on the beliefs and spiritual values of others. Rather, they are encouraged to understand that different perspectives exist and can be respected without the loss of their own spirituality.

At the core, youth practitioners establish cultural safety by examining their own cultural identities and beliefs and by seeking to understand their own attitudes toward people with other cultural practices. It is easy to identify what is different and the same about another person (e.g., celebrations of holidays, worshipping, childrearing practices). It is much more difficult to understand how deeply culture shapes how people think, feel, and behave.

Emotional Safety

Young people experience emotional safety when they are encouraged to identify and express their emotions without judgment or harm. In such contexts, they learn that there are no right or wrong feelings. Youth practitioners support the feeling of emotional safety by creating environments where young people are protected from emotional manipulation, coercion, or threats. The sense of emotional safety also can be strengthened by engaging young people in activities that support the development of emotional and behavioral regulation.

Social Safety

The young person is encouraged to form safe, respectful relationships with adults and peers and is protected from oppressive, coercive, or hurtful people. Social safety is strengthened when adults help young people restore broken relationships and engage with them using the seven habits of caring relationships: trust, attention, empathy, availability, affirmation, respect, and challenge and support.

Practice 4—Engage

The intentional adult is now ready to engage the young person or group of young people. Symbolically, the adult reaches out an open hand to invite the young person to become involved. The invitation is a commitment from the adult to stay engaged with the young person, no matter how tough it might be. It can be very challenging if the young person uses hurtful language or actions. Engagement requires that the adult figures out what the young person needs and how to make it possible for the youth to accept the invitation.

An invitation to engage is in sharp contrast to exclusion, isolation, and sending kids away, even to a timeout. During time of acute stress, the presence of supportive people results in faster recovery. Young people supported by caring adults during times of distress become more trusting of others, more cooperative and social, and they show more trustworthy behaviors than those who are sent away or left to themselves.[232] Once a young person accepts the invitation, a collaborative alliance is established, built on mutual respect and trust.

Engage the Young Person's Deep Brain

Young people, including very young people, are experts in their own lives and can tell what is going on in their brains and spirits.[233] When youth practitioners engage a young person by showing an interest and a desire to understand how he or she sees and acts in the world, the young person's sense of identity and control is strengthened. In this situation, the adult becomes a collaborative partner, rather than an expert who notices and reflects on the young person's feelings, experiences, and words. They tune in to the young people's interests, what calms them, what makes them happy, and what excites them. As a result, adults strengthen their ability to recognize the young person's bids to connect and participate. The young person feels understood because his or her views are taken seriously. This alliance opens the door to the inside kid. The adult can see what's strong, rather than what's wrong and can know that the child would if he or she could. This is important for all kids but especially for kids who have experienced toxic stress.

Young people do well when they can, and when they can't, youth practitioners teach them how. This strengths-based stance assumes that young people do the best they can at any given time because they are wired to meet growth needs, not cause themselves pain. It helps to think that kids always cooperate, even when it does not look like it. Learning to reframe resistance as an attempt to cooperate is an intentional adult capability. Once youth practitioners assume that the young people would if they could, the adult no longer must "fight" the children and their brains. Instead, they can join forces with the young people to move forward.

Engage the Young Person's Character Strengths

During times of stress and challenges, the youth practitioner reminds the young person of what's strong, not of what's wrong. When both the youth and the adult know the young person's strengths, they can be used as pathways toward well-being.

Young people do not need to be in crisis for us to give feedback and draw on their strengths. The more we notice, name, and encourage the use of strengths as a way of being with young people, the more they will engage and achieve positive outcomes. When youth practitioners actively "feed" young people the nourishment their brains need, they strengthen their resilience and shift their scale toward positive outcomes. This was demonstrated by a teacher who used her knowledge of a student's character strength to turn resistance into cooperation.

> It was challenging for John to sit down immediately when class started. Every morning he began the day by greeting friends and chatting, even after being asked to sit down. Instead of seeing this as disobedience, the teacher recognized that John needed to connect with friends before starting class.
>
> The teacher talked with John after class and acknowledged his character strength of social intelligence. She suggested that John spend the first five minutes each morning in welcoming the other kids and asking how they are doing. When prompted by the teacher, John was given the

responsibility to encourage the other students to take their seats and focus on getting ready to participate.

Engage the Young Person's Executive Functions

When young people participate in a conversation with words, their thinking brains are engaged, and they can tap into their executive functions. Youth practitioners can enhance the opportunity for young people to exercise their executive functions by asking open-ended questions. As young people begin to reflect and respond to the questions, they build connections in their brains. Through repeated opportunities to reflect and think, these connections become stronger and easier to access.

Is My Room Clean Now?

> La'Toya, who lives with a foster carer, Nadine, has not been able to clean her room to Nadine's expectations. When Nadine asked her to explain what a clean room looks like, La'Toya looked clueless. Nadine, through questioning and probing, facilitated that La'Toya developed a checklist describing each step and task involved. Through this process, La'Toya exercised the executive function called organize materials. When the list was completed and agreed upon, Nadine checked for understanding by asking La'Toya to repeat the steps without looking at the list, an exercise in working memory. After this, La'Toya was ready to clean her room. At little later, she called Nadine. "Is my room clean now?" It did not meet Nadine's expectations. Rather than becoming frustrated, Nadine realized that La'Toya did not know how to complete the task. She worked with La'Toya and showed her what it means to have a clean room. When they were done, they celebrated their work with high-fives. La'Toya happily said she could now clean her room. Nadine suggested that La'Toya take a picture with her phone so she would have a visual

reminder. This was a way to support La'Toya's exercise task monitoring and to strengthen their relationship.

Engage the Young Person's Deep Culture

Responsive youth practitioners make every effort to relate to the young person's deep culture because it calms the threat-safety detection system. The first step in becoming culturally responsive is to develop an awareness of our own culture.[234] This involves accessing our own deep culture, including our worldview and values.

One of the privileges—and disadvantages—of participating in a dominant culture is that the person is rarely asked about his or her deep culture. In a recent course, a youth practitioner shared with me that many of the children and families with whom he worked had beliefs and behaviors that were very different from his own. He gave several examples and then acknowledged that until that moment, he had never thought that they might say the same about him. Before we rejoined the group, he ended by saying that the scariest thing was that he had no awareness of his own cultural practices and beliefs.

Youth practitioners can begin their journey toward cultural responsiveness by asking themselves questions about their own deeply help beliefs and the cultural practices, as discussed in chapter 11. When youth practitioners become aware of their own deep culture, they either may be comfortable or uncomfortable with what they find. If they begin to change their deeply held values, it can become contagious.

Practice 5—Empower

Empower consists of three responsive practices known by the acronym RAP: (1) reframe and refocus, (2) acknowledge exceptional behavior, and (3) plan and practice for the desired future.

RAP focuses on strengths and finding solutions to pressing issues. It may last as little as fifteen minutes or stretch over several months. It involves three empowerment strategies that flow naturally in an organic dialogue with a young person. The strategies can be used together or individually and can be taught to and practiced by young people. The youth practitioner uses open-ended questions and dialogue to identify the young person's preferences. The basic premise of the RAP is the following:

- Engage young people with a learner's mind, conveying curiosity and not knowing everything or already having the answers.
- Ask many questions, and listen before offering suggestions.
- Respect young people who reject your suggestions. Test different ideas.
- Involve young people in decisions that affect their lives.

Reframe and Refocus

Reframing or refocusing changes the perspective or the way a situation is viewed. It invites different explanations and interpretations of a situation.

People integrate their life experiences into stories that help them understand themselves and explain events in their lives.[235] Children and youth who have experienced toxic stress may develop life stories that attribute bad events to them—they see the events as being their fault or occurring because they are "bad persons." Their mental maps have filtered their experiences and generated the belief that they have no control over their lives and that they do not deserve a good life. This often becomes a self-fulfilling prophecy.

I Have Grown into a Strong and Healthy Person

> Patrick, a young person I knew, told his story this way: "When I was born, my mom left me in the restroom at a Greyhound bus station. I am a piece of shit. You can't trust others. Life sucks, and I don't deserve to live." Patrick and I met regularly over several months, and he began to understand that he had not made his mother leave him in the restroom. He learned to change his viewing of his life and changed his life story to this: "Even though I was left in the restroom at a bus station at birth, I have grown

> into a strong and healthy person. I do well in school and hope to become a mechanic. And have kids of my own" (big smile).

Supportive adults who tap into young people's strengths, relationships, and culture can help them discover underlying, underemphasized themes in their stories that may be helpful in changing the perspective. When we hold a kaleidoscope steady and gaze through it, the colors and shapes remain stationary, but when we turn it, we see new constellations. Similarly, when young people are stuck in one version of their life stories, youth practitioners can help each discover other attributes to create an authentic and different story. The new story will not eliminate the pain but will balance it with strengths, capacities, and the buffers they forged during adversity. Young people may discover that the stress they experienced was not their fault and that they, at times, responded with courage, resourcefulness, and determination.

Hold On to the Medicine Pouch whenever You Need Me

> Hakan, a Native American student in Mr. Munson's class, had been sexually and physically abused at a very young age and currently lived with a foster carer. One day, when he was teased by other students, he began yelling and lifted his shirt, showing the scars left from the abuse. "None of you knows what it's like to be me. None of you was ever beaten like me."
>
> As he calmed down, he told Mr. Munson, "You are the only person I can trust. I know you will never hurt me."
>
> The next day, Mr. Munson caught Hakan stealing items from his backpack. He became very upset and was ready to call the police. After reflecting on the event with other teachers and me, Mr. Munson realized it was possible that Hakan wanted to have something of Mr. Munson's to make him feel safe and loved. With this new perspective, Mr. Munson gave Hakan a medicine pouch and told him,

> "Hold on to medicine pouch whenever you need me, and imagine that my love and support is inside the pouch."
>
> When Mr. Munson visited Hakan in a treatment center a year later, he learned the medicine pouch may have saved Hakan's life. The staff told him that Hakan clutched the medicine pouch during severe times of depression and kept repeating that Mr. Munson loved him. Without the pouch, the staff believed, he might not have pulled through.

To help a young person develop a different life story, adults must be curious, suspend their own cultural lenses, and have a vocabulary of strengths so they can name young people's strengths when they show up. Without a strength language, we are unlikely to detect strengths and could miss the opportunity to teach young people to use their strengths purposefully.

Externalizing Problems

Externalizing a problem or challenging behavior is a special form of reframing.[236] The ability to self-regulate is often disrupted by stress, and many children get stuck in the fight-flight-or-freeze response. As their pain is rarely understood, the young person, in the eyes of others, becomes the problem. Now the young person is angry, explosive, withdrawn, or depressed. Over time, emotional states become traits. In other words, the person has internalized the problem (e.g., I am angry, I am depressed, I am useless). At times, reframing internalized problems as external to the young person can be helpful. [237]

Standing Up to the Terminator

Thirteen-year-old Brian had a long history of neglect and both physical and sexual abuse. He also had one of the shortest fuses I have seen in my classroom. Within seconds, he could change from a hard-working student to a raging volcano, spewing profanities and threats and throwing every item within reach at people, around the room, or through windows. In a calm moment, I invited him to talk about his rage.

Brian: I can't help it.

Me: You can't help it? I need your help to understand that.

Brian: It just happens. You probably don't believe me, but it just happens. I know it is bad. I want to stop it, but it just happens.

Me: That must be hard for you, especially because you want to stop it.

Brian: Yes, I don't know what to do.

Me: Can you help me understand what it's like when it happens?

Brian: I will be working on an assignment, and it's a little bit hard, and it's like someone says, "Brian, just start to scream and throw things around. Just do it."

Brian and I talked a bit about his desire to stop his destructive behaviors and his inability to do so. I then invited him to think about his situation in a different way.

Me: It is almost like something is telling you it's OK to yell and throw stuff around, even though you know it's bad, and you want to stop it. That must be really hard.

Brian: Yes.

Me: I wonder if that *something* is nice or is someone who doesn't care about you.

Brian: It's mean.

Me: Well, I think you are being pushed around by something or someone who does not care about you.

Brian: Yes.

Me: What do you think that thing looks like?

Brian: A monster!

Me: Is it big or small?

Brian: Big.

Me: Does it have a name?

Brian: The Terminator.

Brian and I explored how he could beat the Terminator. We decided that it would take a team, including his parents, an uncle, and two of his friends. Brian was determined to beat the Terminator, and his goal was to develop courage and bravery to tame the Terminator. With this reframe, Brian and his team began to develop strategies and skills to control the Terminator.

Acknowledge Exceptional Behavior

> There are always exceptions to every generalization.
>
> —a Christian epilogue

Solution-focused practices assert that problems do not happen all the time.[238] The second RAP strategy helps the young person discover situations when a problem or challenge did not exist. When the problem does not happen, the young person uses exceptional behavior or exceptional thinking. The youth practitioner and the young person explore when a problem is not happening or happens in a different way or to a lesser degree. In fact, when you consider a day or a week, most problems happen only occasionally. When you find exceptions, affirm the young person with phrases like, "That's a good example of your *exceptional behavior* or *exceptional thinking.*" Also check to affirm that the young person feels less overwhelmed when the problem does not happen. Next, turn your energy to explore the solutions the young person or others already use. The power in finding exceptional behaviors and thinking is that the young person realizes that he or she already has solutions to the problem. With this awareness, he or she can do more of the solution.

Exceptional behaviors and solutions can be found through solution-focused questioning and listening for window words. Exceptional behaviors and thinking also happen when young people use their character strengths or executive functions. Exception questions include the following:

- Tell me about times when the problem is less troubling or when it doesn't happen at all.
- Tell me about when you cope a little bit better.
- What's different when the problem's not there?
- When things are tough, how do you cope?
- Tell me what's worked in the past, even if it's only for a short time. What else?

Listening to the words young people and others use can help detect exceptions. Earlier, we discussed how to listen for window words as used in these examples:

- Most adults don't understand me.
- Sasha rarely completes her chores.
- I hate all my classes, except technology.
- Jason is almost always late for work.

I Would Forgive Him because He Will Always Be My Father

Gabriella, with whom I worked, demonstrated exceptional thinking by using her signature strengths.

> Gabriella was born in the United States to illegal immigrants from Colombia. At age twelve, she gave birth to her father's child and Child Protective Services became involved. Gabriella's dad fled the United States and went back to Colombia to escape prosecution. Her

mother remained in the United States but lost custody of Gabriella and her baby girl, who were both placed in foster care. Missing her parents, Gabriella ran away from the foster carer's home many times and was eventually sent to a residential program at age fifteen, where I met her. During the first several months, she attempted to push every supportive adult away. She slowly began to trust staff after she was connected to a mentor from Chile, partly because they both spoke Spanish.

I met with Gabriella weekly, and we mostly talked about her hopes for the future. We also talked about how she could best apply her signature strengths, which were love of learning, forgiveness, courage, curiosity, and perseverance.

When she was ready to return to the community, I asked her if there was one thing she would like to do if she had the power. Without hesitation, she said, "I would go to Colombia and find my father and tell him I have become strong. I would tell him that it was not my fault I became pregnant and that it was wrong what he did. And then I would forgive him because he will always be my father. That would set me free. Without that, I will continue to be angry."

Intentional Strengths Discovery

If a young person is stuck and unable to see any solutions, there is a different approach to discover exceptions. The adult with the strongest relationship with the young person asks if the young person is willing to participate in an experiment that involves him or her doing three things. First, one day during the next week, the young person must try to be his or her absolute best—socially, emotionally, academically. Second, the young person cannot tell anyone which day he or she is trying his or her best. At the end of the week, the young person writes about his or her best day, giving examples. The adult who arranges the experiment meets with the team of youth practitioners involved with the young person and explains the experiment. Each team member's task is to note individually all the positive acts of the youth each day and write them down. At the end of the week, each team member identifies the day the youth showed the most positive behaviors. Finally, the team and the youth get together and share the results of the experiment.

The result of this intentional strength-finding practice is always amazing! Typically, team members name different days as the youth's strengths day, and rarely does the team pick the day the student reported as his or her strengths day. Over the course of the week, the team searched for strengths and gained a different picture of the young person. This allowed them to see the young person in a new way. When the youth practitioners share their observations, they affirm the young person and find new ways to engage.

Plan the Desired Future

When young people describe their hopes for the future, they create memories of the future, as described earlier. The desired future can be an hour from now, later in the day, a week from now, or next year. It depends on the situation. The desired future does not have to be totally realistic. Encourage the young person to dream and to think big. Solution-focused practitioners often use a version of the miracle question to help arrive at a description of the desired future. The miracle question was inspired by Erick Erickson's crystal ball technique and was developed to help people envision the future: "Suppose that one night, while you were asleep, there was a miracle, and this problem was solved. How would you know? What would be different?"[239] Young people typically find the question enjoyable because it helps them to describe their hopes for the future.

Spotlight 10. The Miracle Question

- If a miracle happened, and your problems went away, how would you and others know?
- If a genie visited you while you were sleeping and wiped out your problems, what would you notice? What would you see? Hear? Do? Feel?
- If this was a magic ball that could tell your future, what would you see?
- If you were beamed to another planet, what would be the first thing you would see when you arrived?
- If you had special powers to make the very best come true, what would you change first?
- What would you like to happen tomorrow?
- What do you hope your teacher will do when you get to school?
- How would you know that something was different about yourself and your situation?
- What would others notice that was different about you, your feelings, and your strengths? What would you be doing? Saying? Feeling?

Current Situation

Once the young person has a vivid idea and image about the desired future, the youth practitioner facilitates the young person to assess how far he or she is from being there. Since we have already identified solutions and exceptions, we assume progress. We encourage young people to describe where they are now—their current situations—in relation to the desired future.

Scaling questions are useful in identifying the current situation. For example, a young person whose desired future is passing all classes in school may use a scale where 0 means failing all classes, and 10 means passing all classes. To make the scale useful, facilitate the development of the meaning of other points on the scale; for example, 5 means passing language arts and math, and 7 means also passing science. Encourage the young person to be realistic, so he or she will experience success. The answer may be, "I will work as hard as I can to pass history and art this semester." You also can use tangible things to anchor the scale, such as 1 being a bicycle, 5 a Ford, and 10 a Ferrari. You can then ask which vehicle the child drives now and what it would take to get an upgrade.

The exploration of the desired future and the current situation is a goal-setting process that focuses on doing something rather than stopping to do something—developing a list of what the young person wants to do. Fredrike Bannink provided this comparison: "If you go to the supermarket, do you want to make a list of the things you want to buy, or a list of the things you don't want to buy? If you chose the latter, that would mean making a list of about 5,000 things you didn't want to buy. Of course, you'll make a list of what you do want. For that same reason, ask a person what they want instead of what they don't want."[240]

When the young person has described the desired future and current situation, we explore how he or she and others will know that the future has been achieved. We use open-ended questions like these:

- What will be the first thing you notice tomorrow morning that will tell you that you are closer to achieving your goal?
- What would you like to be different two weeks from now?
- How will you know you are different three months from now?
- What would you do instead of (failing classes, getting into fights, losing your temper)?
- How will your (mom/dad/teacher/youth worker) know that you are there?
- How will your friends know you can be trusted? What will that feel like?
- What will you do/say?

The Stranger, a wise character in *Winnie-the-Pooh on Success*, gives Pooh and his friends the acronym SUCCESS to help them remember what it takes to achieve their desired future.[241]

- *S*elect a dream.
- *U*se your dreams to set a goal.
- *C*reate a plan.
- *C*onsider resources.
- *E*nhance skills and abilities.
- *S*pend time wisely.
- *S*tart—get organized and go.

Practice for the Desired Future for Positive Outcomes

> I have not failed. I've just found 10,000 ways that don't work.
>
> —Thomas A. Edison

> I've missed more than nine thousand shots in my career. I've lost almost three hundred games. Twenty-six times, I've been trusted to take the game-winning shot and missed. I've failed over and over again in my life. And that is why I succeed.
>
> —Michael Jordan

Young people need intentional environments and supportive adults to achieve their desired future and positive outcomes. Thomas A. Edison and Michael Jordan highlighted that success comes from practice. Angela Duckworth's extensive research on grit and self-control has shown how these contribute to successful outcomes.[242] In fact, grit is a better predictor of success than grade point average and IQ. Grit is the "perseverance to accomplish long-term or higher-order goals in the face of challenges and setbacks, engaging the student's psychological resources, such as their academic mind-sets, effortful control, and strategies and tactics."[243]

Supporting and nurturing young people to develop resilience and well-being are essential to achieving success.

Practice 6—Responsive Environments

Young people live in interwoven social contexts known as the social ecology. The ecology can provide rich, protective, positive relationships to complement the child. On the other hand, a poorly resourced ecology, with few or negative relationships, can undermine growth and be hurtful and overwhelming.

Young people live their social lives within four interacting contexts: the school, the home/family, the community, and cyberspace.[244] Other contexts exist, including youth groups, the streets, gangs, religious communities, and sports teams. In traditional territories, relatedness includes people, wildlife, ancestors, and vegetation. Together, these contexts comprise the young person's social ecology.

Understanding the relatedness of young people across their social ecology enables youth practitioners to go beyond an isolated observation in, for example, a classroom to understand a young person. This offers a deeper and broader understanding of the young person across the various contexts in which he or she functions. A fight between parents in the home may result in an angry reaction to a teacher the next day. Young people who have been bullied in cyberspace may take their hurt out on a sibling or ignore a simple request from a parent to do their chores. Conversely, a positive relationship and positive experiences in one context can serve as a buffer in a less positive context. Resolving a conflict at school and getting encouragement for taking leadership can result in courage to say no when confronted with pressure. Kindness and compassion shown by parents to a child who causes an upset at home may enable the child to show compassion when a fellow student forgets his or her homework and needs assistance at school.

The social and physical ecologies are vital to health and well-being, including social-emotional, psychological, behavioral, cognitive, and physical outcomes across child and adolescent development. Individual and communitywide efforts are vital to develop places where youth can thrive. Though none of us can change all the places where young people grow up, remember that a little change leads to more change. It takes just a few people to start a movement! You can influence the environments where you engage with young people—in schools, in the community and sports programs, in residential facilities, in your own home, and in the homes of families and friends.

I offer a set of principles that are essential in responsive environments:

- Prioritize relationship and relatedness.
- Become culturally responsive.
- Sustain safety across all dimensions for children and adults.
- Nurture character strengths and executive functions.
- Promote achievement of psychosocial needs.
- Strive to achieve positive outcomes for each young person every day.
- Focus on individuals in the context of the group.
- Focus on the inside kid to influence positive outcomes.
- Be hopeful and positive, and focus on the strong rather than on what's wrong.
- Use responsive practices, and avoid coercion and compliance.
- Encourage, harness, and facilitate the support of prosocial peers and peer groups.
- Expand awareness and support of positive use of cyberspace and connections.

Reflections

- Reframe a personal challenge to change your viewing of the challenge.
- Find exceptions to a personal challenge. Begin doing more of the exception.

- Talk to a young person about his or her desired future, and help him or her make the image stick.
- What is one thing you can do to make your environment more supportive for young people?

Explorations

- Review the website for the Institute for Solution-Focused Therapy at https://solution.net/what-is-solution-focused-therapy/.
- Read *Brief Coaching with Children and Young People: A Solution-Focused Approach* by Harvey Ratner and Denise Yussef.[245]
- Read *Working with High-Risk Adolescents: An Individualized Family Therapy Approach* by Matthew Selekman.[246]

Appendices

Appendix A. Description of Negative Outcomes

Negative Outcomes	Pain-Based Emotions	Pain-Based Thinking	Pain-Based Behaviors
Loss of relationship, identity, and security	Sadness, detachment, anger, unhappiness, anxiety, fear, lost, depression, confusion.	I can't trust them. I must get them before they get me. I'm a failure. I'm not lovable. I don't know who I am and where I fit.	Withdrawal, unable to concentrate or learn, disengaged, poor choice of friends and peer groups, verbal lashing out, physical lashing out, relationship reluctance, self-harm, unable to express strengths, gang involvement, negative or unhealthy relationships, rejection of cultural traditions
Inability to learn and adapt	Frustration; feeling stupid, incompetent, anxious, confused, fearful, stressed, ashamed	I'm stupid. I'll never … It's not worth trying. I can't. It's their fault. It's too hard.	Bullying, disengaged from school and learning, lack of concentration, crying, verbal aggression, avoidance, withdrawal, agitation, unable to compete tasks, putting others down, indecisiveness, unable to solve problems
Inability to self-regulate	Overwhelmed; out of control; feeling anxious, angry, frustrated, powerless, depressed, foolish, agitated, humiliated	It's not my fault. It's them. It's your fault. Make me. Just this once … I can't help it.	Emotional outbursts, thoughtless actions, bullying, overindulgence, easily influenced, verbal or physical aggression, breaking things, stealing, lying, refusal, self-harm, controlling, poor choices, unwilling to accept consequence, unable to express strengths, prejudice, discrimination, self-indulgence

Negative Outcomes	Pain-Based Emotions	Pain-Based Thinking	Pain-Based Behaviors
Disengaged and without purpose	Despair; feeling insignificant, lost, afraid, lonely, sad, angry, anxious, helpless powerless	Why should I? Who needs me? I don't matter. It's not my problem. I've got nothing to offer. It won't change anything.	Withdrawn, self-absorbed, involved in isolated activities, involved with harmful causes, aimless, unable to focus and concentrate, lacking in energy, unable to express strengths, indifferent to others
Hopelessness	Fearful, depressed, lonely, sad, unhappy, desperate	I don't care. Nothing ever changes. No one cares. Why bother?	Withdrawal, damaging property, stealing, substance abuse, aggression toward others, refusal to help others, self-harm, disengaged
Harm to self or others	Anger, rage, desperation, pain, powerlessness, depression, hopelessness	I'll get them. If I hurt them first ... It doesn't matter. This will never go away. I don't want to feel like this. I can end this. No thought	Suicidal, substance abuse, cutting or choking self, breaking things, verbal abuse toward others, negative self-talk, physical aggression, range involvement, involvement in negative causes, withdrawal, prejudice, unable to accept others, selfish
Unhealthy brain functioning	Lost, afraid, incompetent, overwhelmed, confused, agitated, fearful exhausted, depressed	Inability to think straight No thought I can't. I don't want to. What's wrong with me?	Emotional outbursts, unable to complete tasks, harm to self and others, inability to concentrate and learn, inability to self-regulate, inability to choose or solve problems
Physical ailments	Pain, desperation, hopelessness, helplessness, anger, frightened, overwhelmed		

Negative Outcomes	Pain-Based Emotions	Pain-Based Thinking	Pain-Based Behaviors
Mental illness	Sad, depressed, frustrated, isolated, stupid, helpless, hopeless, overwhelmed, anxious, confused, enraged, angry	I don't know how. I'm a freak. I'm stupid. I'll never … They won't help me. No one can help me. Don't know how … I'm a freak. I'm stupid. I'll never … Inability to think straight	Withdrawal, self-harm substance abuse, self-medication, aimlessness, homelessness, unable to find employment, on the streets, involved in unhealthy causes or gangs, violence, hurtful to others, poor concentration, agitation

Appendix B. Description of Positive Outcomes

Positive Outcomes	Positive Emotions	Positive Thinking	Positive Behaviors
To belong in an ecology of relatedness	Safe, secure, loved, happy, warmth, gratitude, joy, encouraged, confident, proud	I'm safe. I matter. I belong. They can help. I'm not alone. I'm OK.	Kindness, empathy, expression of warmth and love, cooperation, participation, leadership, positive relationships, social awareness and skills, respecting others, trusting others, caring for the environment, teamwork, expression of cultural traditions and values
Achievement of goals and coping with challenges	Comfortable, capable, strong, positive, hopeful, encouraged, proud, confident, courageous, knowledgeable, successful, influential	I can. I will. I want to. I'm able. It can change. There are always exceptions. I can influence ... The solution is ...	Learns, has curiosity, has creativity, has concentration, focuses, plans, participates, collaborates, makes positive decisions, finds solutions, problem solves, seeks knowledge, perseveres, completes tasks, takes on new challenges, adapts to change and transition, demonstrates social skill
Autonomy to regulate emotions and actions	In control, confident, capable, independent, good, trust of self, respected, energized, motivated, proud	I'm able. I'm in control of me. I don't need to control or hurt. I can choose. I'm responsible. I'm accountable. I can change.	Makes careful choices Considers consequences before acting Takes responsibility Manages emotions Thinks before reacting Exercises prudence Takes charge of self Self-aware Resists influence Resists overindulgence Exercises good judgment
Contribution to others and the community	Good, appreciated, needed, satisfied, useful, competent, belonging, joyful, fulfilled	I can cooperate. I can make a difference. I'm important. I matter. I belong.	Helpful, performs acts of kindness, expresses empathy and compassion, contributes to collective activities and goals, teamwork, courageous, provides perspective, participation, collaboration, generosity, can set aside own needs for those of others, cares for the land, has social intelligence, fairness, fights for justice

Positive Outcomes	Positive Emotions	Positive Thinking	Positive Behaviors
Hope and purpose	Positive, hopeful, optimistic, encouraged, motivated, interested, calm, joyful, belonging.	I'll get there. This can change. It's worth it. My dream is … There's a bigger picture. There's meaning to this. It can work.	Provides positive perspective, perseveres, makes changes, expresses faith and cultural traditions, dreams, participates in meaningful activities, spirituality, takes on new challenges, works to find solutions to problems
Well-being	Positive, hopeful, encouraged, motivated, joyful, content, confident, competent, belonging, trust, happy, grateful, strong, optimistic	Life is good. Everything's worthwhile in the end. All of the above	The expression of character strengths All of the above

Appendix C. Hofstede's Dimensions of National Culture

Power Distance

The degree to which the less powerful members of a society accept and expect that power is distributed unequally and how inequalities among people are addressed

People in societies with a large degree of power distance accept a hierarchy. In societies with low power distance, people strive to equalize the distribution of power and demand justification for inequalities of power.

Individualism versus Collectivism

Individualism reflects a preference for a loosely knit social framework in which individuals are expected to take care of only themselves and their immediate families. Collectivism refers to a preference for a tightly knit framework in society in which individuals can expect their relatives or members of an in-group to look after them in exchange for unquestioning loyalty. A society's position on this dimension is reflected in whether people's self-image is defined in terms of "I" or "we."

Masculinity versus Femininity

Masculinity represents a preference in society for achievement, heroism, assertiveness, and material rewards for success. Society at large is mostly competitive. Femininity reflects a preference for cooperation, modesty, caring for the weak, and quality of life. Society at large is more consensus-oriented.

Uncertainty Avoidance

Uncertainty avoidance is the degree to which the members of a society feel uncomfortable with uncertainty and ambiguity. The fundamental question is this: Should we try to control the future or just let it happen?

Countries with high uncertainty avoidance maintain rigid codes of belief and behavior and are intolerant of unorthodox behavior and ideas. Weak uncertainty-avoidance societies maintain a more relaxed attitude, in which practice counts more than principles.

Long-Term Orientation versus Short-Term Orientation

Every society maintains some links with its own past while dealing with the challenges of the present and the future.

Societies with a long-term orientation prefer time-honored traditions and norms while viewing societal change with suspicion. Those with a short-term orientation prefer flexibility and innovation.

Indulgence versus Restraint

Societies with a preference for indulgence allow relatively free gratification of basic and natural human drives related to enjoying life and having fun. Restraint stands for a society that suppresses gratification of needs and regulates it by means of strict social norms.

Adapted from https://www.hofstede-insights.com/models/national-culture/

Index

A

B

C

D

E

F

G

H

R

S

T

U

V

W

Y

Notes

1 Adapted from Loren Eiseley, *The Star Thrower* (New York: Harvest Books, 1979).

2 Wayne McCashen, *The Strengths Approach: A Strengths-Based Resource for Sharing Power and Creating Change* (Bendigo: St Luke's Innovative Resources, 2005).

3 Erik K. Laursen, "Strengths-Based Practice with Children in Trouble," *Reclaiming Children and Youth* 11, no. 2 (Spring 2002): 70–75.

4 Dennis Saleebey, *The Strengths Perspective in Social Work Practice* (Upper Saddle River: Pearson, 2012).

5 McCashen, *The Strengths Approach: A Strengths-Based Resource for Sharing Power and Creating Change,* 9

6 Laursen, "Strengths-Based Practice."

7 See, for example, Fredrike Bannink, *Post-Traumatic Success: Positive Psychology and Solution-Focused Strategies to Help Clients Survive and Thrive* (New York: W. W. Norton, 2014); Steve de Shazer and Yvonne Dolan, *More than Miracles: The State of the Art of Solution-Focused Brief Therapy* (New York: Haworth Press, 2007); John J. Murphy, *Solution-Focused Counseling in Schools* (Alexandria: American Counseling Organization, 2013).

8 Italics from Matthew D. Selekman, *Pathways to Change: Brief Therapy Solutions with Difficult Adolescents* (New York: Guilford Press, 1993), 25–44.

9 Positive Psychology Center. Accessed December 9, 2017. https://ppc.sas.upenn.edu; International Positive Psychology Association, accessed August 12, 2016, http://www.ippanetwork.org.

10 Martin E. P. Seligman and Mihaly Csikszentmihalyi, "Positive Psychology: An Introduction," *American Psychologist* 56, no. 1 (2000): 6, http://doi.org/10.1037/0003-066X.55.1.5.

11 Christopher Peterson, "What Is Positive Psychology and What Is It Not?" *Psychology Today,* March 16, 2008, https://www.psychologytoday.com/blog/the-good-life/200805/what-is-positive-psychology-and-what-is-it-not.

12 Seligman and Csikszentmihalyi, "Positive Psychology," 6.

13 Shelly L. Gable and Jonathan Haidt. "What (and Why?) Is Positive Psychology?" *Review of General Psychology* 9, no. 2 (2005): 103, https://doi.org/10.1037/1089-2680.9.2.103.

14 Positive Psychology Institute. "What is Positive Psychology?" Accessed May 12, 2016. http://www.positivepsychologyinstitute.com.au/what_is_positive_psychology.html.

15 Paul T. P. Wong et al. *The Positive Psychology of Meaning and Spirituality: Selected Papers from Meaning Conferences* (Birmingham: Purpose Research, 2012).

16 Martin E. P. Seligman, *Flourish: A Visionary New Understanding of Happiness and Well-Being* (New York: Free Press, 2011), 16–20.

17 Center on the Developing Child at Harvard University. *The Science of Resilience.* Issue Brief. 2015. https://46y5eh11fhgw3ve3ytpwxt9r-wpengine.netdna-ssl.com/wp-content/uploads/2015/05/InBrief-The-Science-of-Resilience.pdf.

18 Martin Seligman, "The New Era of Positive Psychology." TED video, 23:48. Posted 2004. https://www.ted.com/talks/martin_seligman_on_the_state_of_psychology.

19 UM News Service, "Christopher Peterson: What Makes Life Worth Living? (Part 1)" You Tube video, 4:30. Posted October 18 2011, https://www.youtube.com/watch?v=DRiIAqGXLKA.

UM News Service, "Christopher Peterson: What makes life worth living? (Part 2)." You Tube Video, 3:49. Posted October 18, 2011, https://www.youtube.com/watch?v=SvZQsqHVjHU.

20 Martin E. P. Seligman et al, "Positive Education: Positive Psychology and Classroom Interventions," *Oxford Review of Education* 35, no. 3 (2009): 293–311, https://doi.org/ 10.1080/03054980902934563.

21 Christopher Peterson, *A Primer in Positive Psychology* (Oxford: Oxford University Press, 2006).

22 Ricardo Arguís Rey. "The Future of Happiness." YouTube video, 15:46. Posted January 16, 2012. www.youtube.com/watch?v=ARcB9KUdv9M.

23 Ricardo Arguís Rey et al. *The "Happy Classrooms" Programme: Positive Psychology Applied to Education.* (Author, 2014). http://educaposit.blogspot.com/p/free-programme-download.html

24 For Maslow's Hierarchy of Needs, see Abraham H. A. Maslow, *A Theory of Human Motivation* (Eastfort: Martino Fine Books, 2013). For Maslow's unpublished revision of the Hierarchy of Needs, see Mark E. Koltko-Rivera, "Rediscovering the Later Version of Maslow's Hierarchy of Needs: Self-Transcendence and Opportunities for Theory, Research, and Unification," *Review of General Psychology* 10, no. 4 (2006): 302–317. https://dor.org/10.1037/1089-2680.10.4.302.

25 Center on the Developing Child at Harvard University. *The Science of Resilience.*

26 Seligman, *Flourish,* 16–20.

27 Karen Johnson Pittman et al., *Preventing Problems, Promoting Development, Encouraging Engagement: Competing Priorities or Inseparable Goals* (Washington, DC: The Forum for Youth Investment, Impact Strategies, March 2003), https://www.forumfyi.org.

28 Richard M. Lerner, *The Good Teen: Rescuing Adolescence from the Myth of the Storm and Stress Years* (New York: Crown, 2007).

29 Larry K. Brendtro and Leslie D. du Toit, *Response Ability Pathways: Restoring Bonds of Respect* (Cape Town: Pretext, 2005).

30 Roy F. Baumeister and Mark R. Leary, "The Need to Belong: Desire for Interpersonal Attachments as a Fundamental Human Motivation," *Psychological Bulletin* 117, no. 3 (1995): 497–529.

31 Janis L. Whitlock, "Youth Perceptions of Life at School: Contextual Correlates of School Connectedness in Adolescence," *Applied Developmental Science* 10, no 1. (2010): 13–29, https://10.1207/s1532480xads1001_2.

32 Center on the Developing Child at Harvard University. *The Science of Resilience*; Louis Cozolino, *The Neuroscience of Human Relationships: Attachment and the Developing Social Brain* (New York: Norton, 2014).

33 Center on the Developing Child at Harvard University, *The Science of Resilience*; Norman Garmezy, "Children in Poverty: Resilience Despite Risk," *Psychiatry* 56, no. 1 (1993): 127–136, https://doi.org/10.1080/00332747.1993.11024627; Ann S. Masten, *Ordinary Magic: Resilience in Development.* (New York: The Guilford Press, 2014); Emmy E. Werner and Ruth S. Smith, *Overcoming the Odds: High Risk Children from Birth to Adulthood* (Ithaca: Cornell University Press, 1992).

34 Peter Senge, *The Fifth Discipline: The Art & Practice of the Learning Organization* (New York: Doubleday, 1990), 142.

35 Mihaly Csikszentmihalyi, *Finding Flow: The Psychology of Engagement with Everyday Life* (New York: Basic Books, 1990).

36 Albert Bandura, "Exercise of personal and collective efficacy in changing societies," in *Self-Efficacy and Changing Societies* (New York: Cambridge University Press, 1995), 1–45; Julian B. Rotter, *Social Learning and Clinical Psychology* (Englewood Cliffs: Prentice Hall, 1954).

37 Andras Angyal, in *Neurosis and Treatment: A Holistic Theory*, ed. Eugenia Hanfmann and Richard M. Jones (New York: J. Wiley, 1965), 3–29.

38 Martin Luther King, Jr., in *A Knock at Midnight: Inspiration from the Great Sermons of Reverend Martin Luther King, Jr.*, ed. Clayborne Carson and Peter Holloran (New York: Warner Books, 2000), 182.

39 Martin L. Hoffman, "Is Altruism Part of Human Nature?" *Journal of Personality and Social Psychology* 40, no. 1 (1981): 121–137, http://dx.doi.org/10.1037/0022-3514.40.1.121.

40 Harriet Over and Malinda Carpenter, "Eighteen-Month-Old Infants Show Increased Helping Following Priming with Affiliation," *Psychological Science* 20, no. 10 (October, 2010): 1189–93, http://dx.doi.org/10.1037/0022-3514.40.1.121.

41 Felix Warneken and Michael Tomasello, "Altruistic Helping in Human Infants and Young Chimpanzees," *Science* 311 (March 3, 2006): 1301–03, https://doi.org/10.1111/j.1467-9280.2009.02419.x.

42 Robert Brooks and Sam Goldstein, *Raising Resilient Children: Fostering Strength, Hope, and Optimism in Your Child* (Chicago: Contemporary Books, 2001).

43 Mihaly Csikszentmihalyi, *Finding Flow,* 131.

44 Shane J. Lopez, "Hope is a Strategy," YouTube video, 22:01. Posted January 9, 2014, https://www.youtube.com/watch?v=AXBEoTepQHQ.

45 Emily Esfahani Smith, *The Power of Meaning: Crafting a Life That Matters* (New York: Crown, 2017).

46 Patrick L. Hill and Nicholas A. Turiano, "Purpose in Life as Predictor of Mortality Across Adulthood," *Psychological Science* 25, no. 7 (May 2014): 1482–86, https://doi.org/10.1177/0956797614531799.

47 Shane J. Lopez, *Making Hope Happen: Create the Future You Want for Yourself and Others* (New York: Atria, 2013).

48 Shane J. Lopez, "Hope is a Strategy."

49 Andras Angyal, *Neurosis and Treatment*; Urie Bronfenbrenner, "What Do Families Do?" *Institute for American Values* 2 (Winter/Spring 1991).

50 National Scientific Council on the Developing Child, "Supportive Relationships and Active Skill-Building Strengthen the Foundations of Resilience." Working paper 13 no. 13. 2015. https://46y5eh11fhgw3ve3ytpwxt9r-wpengine.netdna-ssl.com/wp-content/uploads/2015/05/The-Science-of-Resilience2.pdf.

51 Larry K. Brendtro and Martin L. Mitchell, *Deep Brain Learning: Evidence-Based Essentials in Education, Treatment, and Youth Development* (Albion: Circle of Courage/Starr Commonwealth, 2015).

52 Bruce D. Perry and Erin P. Hambrick, "The Neurosequential Model of Therapeutics," *Reclaiming Children and Youth* 17, no. 3 (Fall 2008), 39.

53 Paul D. MacLean, *The Triune Brain in Evolution: Role in Paleocerebral Functions* (New York: Springer, 1990).

54 David A. Sousa, *How the Brain Learns* (Thousand Oaks: Corwin, 2015).

55 Frances E. Jensen and Amy Ellis Nutt, *The Teenage Brain: A Neuroscientist's Survival Guide to Raising Adolescents and Young Adults* (New York: HarperCollins, 2015); Daniel J. Siegel, *Brainstorm: The Power and Purpose of the Teenage Brain* (New York, NY: Penguin, 2013); Lawrence Steinberg, *Age of Opportunity: Lessons from the Science of Adolescence* (Boston: Mariner Books, 2014).

56 Center on the Developing Child at Harvard University, "Serve and Return Shape Brain Circuitry," YouTube video, 1:42. Posted September 29, 2011, https://www.youtube.com/watch?v=m_5u8-QSh6A.

57 Louis Cozolino, *The Neuroscience of Human Relationships: Attachment and the Developing Social Brain* (New York: Norton, 2006); Sousa, *How the Brain Learns;* Steinberg, *Age of Opportunity.*

58 Gerard A. Gioia, Peter K. Isquith, Steven C. Guy, and Lauren Kenworthy, *Rating Inventory of Executive Function* (Lutz: PAR, 2016).

59 Jensen and Nutt, *The Teenage Brain.*

60 Siegel, *Brainstorm*; Steinberg, *How the Brain Learns*; Jensen and Nutt, *The Teenage Brain.*

61 Steinberg, *Age of Opportunity.*

62 Steinberg, *Age of Opportunity.*

63 Sousa, *How the Brain Learns.*

64 Steinberg, *Age of Opportunity.*

65 Liz Murray, *Breaking Night: A Memoir of Forgiveness, Survival, and My Journey from Homeless to Harvard* (New York: Hyperion, 2010).

66 Murray, *Breaking Night.*

67 Murray, *Breaking Night,* 37.

68 Rebecca D. O'Brien, "After Harvard, a New Home," *The Harvard Crimson*, April 14, 2003, http://www.thecrimson.com/article/2003/4/14/after-harvard-a-new-home-the/?page=single; "Liz Murray" in Wikipedia.

69 O'Brien, *The Harvard Crimson*, 5th para., line 7.

70 Joanna Walter, "Liz Murray: My Parents were Desperate Drug Addicts. I'm a Harvard Graduate," *The Guardian*, September 25, 2010, https://www.theguardian.com/world/2010/sep/26/liz-murray-bronx-harvard.

71 Brendtro and du Toit, *Response Ability Pathways*, 5.

72 Brendtro and du Toit, *Response Ability Pathways*, 5.

73 Brendtro and du Toit, *Response Ability Pathways*, 5.

74 Ishmael Beah, *A Long Way Gone: Memoirs of a Boy Soldier* (New York: Sarah Crichton Books, 2007); Waln K. Brown and John Seita, *Growing up in the Care of Strangers: The Experiences, Insights and Recommendations of Eleven Former Foster Kids* (Tallahassee: William Gladden Foundation Press, 2009); Regina Calcaterra, *Etched in Sand: A True Story of Five Siblings Who Survived an Unspeakable Childhood on Long Island* (New York: William Morrow, 2013); Antwone Q. Fisher and Mim E. Rivas, *Finding Fish: A Memoir* (New York: Morrow, 2001); Ashley Rhodes-Courter, *Three Little Words: A Memoir* (New York: Atheneum, 2008).

75 Brian Raychaba, *Pain ... Lots of Pain: Family Violence and Abuse in the Lives of Young People in Care* (Ottawa: National Youth in Care Network, 1993).

76 James P. Anglin, *Pain, Normality and the Struggle for Congruence: Reinterpreting Residential Care for Children and Youth* (New York: Haworth Press, 2002).

77 Joanna Walters, "Liz Murray: My Parents were Desperate Drug Addicts. I'm a Harvard Graduate," *The Guardian*, September 25, 2010, https://www.theguardian.com/world/2010/sep/26/liz-murray-bronx-harvard.

78 Susan Donaldson James, "Homeless to Harvard: Child of Addicts Counsels Youth in Spirituality," *ABC News*, October 10, 2013, http://abcnews.go.com/Health/homeless-harvard-child-addicts-counsels-youth-spirituality/story?id=20523916.

79 James, "Homeless to Harvard," 2nd last paragraph.

80 Walters, "Liz Murray," paragraph 7.

81 Christopher Peterson and Martin E. Seligman, *Character Strengths and Virtues: A Handbook and Classification* (Washington, DC: American Psychological Association, 2004).

82 Bruce D. Perry and Maia Szalavitz, *The Boy Who Was Raised as A Dog: And Other Stories from a Child Psychiatrist's Notebook—What Traumatized Children Can Teach Us About Loss, Love, and Healing* (New York: Basic Books, 2006).

83 Susan A. Craig, *Reaching and Teaching Children Who Hurt: Strategies for Your Classroom* (East Peoria: Brookes Publishing, 2008).

84 Vincent J. Felitti et al., "Relationship of Childhood Abuse and Household Dysfunction to Many of the Leading Causes of Death in Adults," *American Journal of Preventive Medicine* 14, no. 4 (1998): 245–258, http://doi.org/10.1016/s0749-3797(98)00017-8.

85 Felitti et al., "Relationships of Childhood Abuse"; The original ACE survey is available at http://www.ncjfcj.org/sites/default/files/Finding%20Your%20ACE%20Score.pdf.

86 Robert F. Anda and Vincent J. Felitti, "Adverse Childhood Experiences and Their Relationship to Adult Well-Being and Disease: Turning Gold into Lead," last modified August 27, 2012, https://www.thenationalcouncil.org/wp-content/uploads/2012/11/Natl-Council-Webinar-8-2012.pdf.

87 Charles A. Nelson, Nathan A. Fox, and Charles H. Zeanah, *Romania's Abandoned Children: Deprivation, Brain Development, and the Struggle for Recovery* (Cambridge: Harvard University Press, 2014).

88 Wendy R. Ellis and William H. Dietz, "A New Framework for Addressing Adverse Childhood and Community Experiences: The Building Community Resilience Model," *Academic Pediatrics* 17, no. 7 (October 2017): S86–S93, https:/doi.org/10.1016/j.acap.2016.12.011.

89 Data Resource Center for Child and Adolescent Health, 2016 *National survey of children's health*. Accessed February 14, 2017 from http://www.childhealthdata.org/learn/NSCH.

90 Data Resource Center for Child and Adolescent Health, 2016 *National survey of children's health.*

91 Data Resource Center for Child and Adolescent Health, 2016 *National survey of children's health.*

92 Kristin Turneya and Christopher Wildeman, "Adverse Childhood Experiences Among Children Placed in and Adopted from Foster Care: Evidence from a Nationally Representative Survey," *Child Abuse and Neglect* 64 (February 2017): 117–29, https://doi.org/10.1016/j.chiabu.2016.12.009.

93 Children's Bureau, The AFCARS Report, *Preliminary FY 2014 Estimates as of July 2015,* No. 22. US Department of Health and Human Services, Administration for Children and Families, Administration on Children, Youth and Families, Washington, DC, July 2015, http://www.acf.hhs.gov/sites/default/files/cb/afcarsreport22.pdf.

94 M. Dolan, C. Casanueva, K. Smith, and H. Ringeisen, *NSCAW Child Well-Being Spotlight: More Than One Quarter of Children Placed Out of Home Experience Placement Disruption in the First 18 Months After a Maltreatment Investigation*, OPRE report #2013-05 (Washington, DC: Office of Planning, Research and Evaluation, Administration for Children and Families, US Department of Health and Human Services, Administration for Children and Families, February 11, 2013); National Resource Center for Permanency and Family Connections, *Placement Stability Information Packet,* US Department of Health and Human Services, Administration for Children and Families, Administration on Children, Youth and Families. Washington, DC, December 2009, http://www.hunter.cuny.edu/socwork/nrcfcpp/info_services/Placement_Stability_Info_Pack.htm.

95 Nadine Burke Harris, Nadine, and T. Renschler, *Center for Youth Wellness ACE-Questionnaire* (San Francisco: Center for Youth Wellness, 2015); Monica Bucci et al., *Center for Youth Wellness ACE-Questionnaire User Guide* (San Francisco, CA: Center for Youth Wellness, 2015); Wendy R. Ellis and William H. Dietz, "A New Framework."

96 *Paper Tigers: One High School's Unlikely Success Story,* directed by James Redford (KPJR Films, 2015), DVD.

97 *Resilience: The Biology of Stress and the Science of Hope,* directed by James Redford (KPJR Films, 2015), DVD.

98 Paul W. Baker and Meredith White-McMahon, *The Hopeful Brain: NeuroRelational Repair for Disconnected Children and Youth* (Lulu Publishing Services, 2014); Louis Cozolino, *The Neuroscience of Education: Optimizing Attachment & Learning in the Classroom* (New York: Norton, 2013); National Scientific Council on the Developing Child, *Persistent Fear and Anxiety Can Affect Young Children's Learning and Development.* Working paper no. 9. 2010, https://46y5eh11fhgw3ve3ytpwxt9r-wpengine.netdna-ssl.com/wp-content/

uploads/2010/05/Persistent-Fear-and-Anxiety-Can-Affect-Young-Childrens-Learning-and-Development.pdf; Bruce D. Perry et al., "Childhood Trauma, the Neurobiology of Adaptation, and 'Use-Dependent' Development of the Brain: How 'States' Become 'Traits.'" *Infant Mental Health Journal* 16, no. 4 (Winter 1995): 271–91, https://doi.org/10.1002/1097-0355(199524)16:4<271::AID-IMHJ2280160404>3.0.CO;2-B; Sousa, *How the Brain Learns;* Bessel van der Kolk, *The Body Keeps the Score: Brain, Mind, and Body in the Healing of Trauma* (New York: Penguin, 2014).

99 Siegel, *Brainstorm.*

100 Perry et al., "Childhood Trauma."

101 René A Spitz, "Anaclitic Depression," in *The Psychoanalytic Study of the Child,* ed. R. S. Eisller (New York: International Universities Press, 1946).

102 Allan N. Schore, *Affect Regulation and the Repair of the Self* (New York: Norton, 2003), 68.

103 Sean M. Smith and Wylie W. Vale, "The Role of The Hypothalamic-Adrenal Axis in Neuroendocrine Responses to Stress," *Dialogues Clinical Neuroscience* 8, no. 4 (February 2006): 383–95, https://www.ncbi.nlm.nih.gov/pmc/articles/PMC3181830/.

104 Bruce D. Perry, "Applying principles of Neurodevelopment to Clinic Work with Maltreated and Traumatized Children," in *Working with Traumatized Youth in Child Welfare,* ed. Nancy Boyd Webb (New York, NY: The Guilford Press, 2006), 32, 27-52.

105 Harvard Health Publications, "Understanding the Stress Response: Chronic Activation of This Survival Mechanism Impairs Health." Last updated March 18, 2016, http://www.health.harvard.edu/staying-healthy/understanding-the-stress-response.

106 "Understanding the Stress Response," Harvard Health Publications.

107 Bessel van der Kolk, *The Body Keeps the Score,* 310.

108 Daniel Goleman, *Emotional Intelligence: Why It Matters More Than IQ* (New York: Bantam Books, 1995).

109 Paul W. Baker and Meredith White McMahon, *The Hopeful Brain.*

110 Nicholas J. Long, Mary M. Wood, and Frank A. Fescer, *Life Space Crisis Intervention: Talking with Students in Conflict* (Austin: Pro-Ed, 2001).

111 Andres Slaby and Lili Frank Garfinkel, *No One Saw My Pain: Why Teens Kill Themselves* (New York: W. W. Norton, 1994).

112 Elizabeth A. Shirtcliff, Christopher L. Coe, and Seth D. Pollak, "Early Childhood Stress Is Associated with Elevated Antibody Levels to Herpes Simplex Virus Type 1," *Proceedings of the National Academy of Sciences* 106, no. 8 (February 2009): 2963–67, https://doi.org/10.1073/pnas.0806660106.

113 Michael J. Meany, "Maternal Care, Gene Expression, and Transmission of Individual Differences in Stress Reactivity Across Generations," *Annual*

Review of Neuroscience, 24 (2001): 1161–92, https://doi.org/10.1146/annurev.neuro.24.1.1161.

114 Sarah E. Romens, Jennifer McDonald, John Svaren, and Seth D. Pollak, "Associations Between Early Life Stress and Gene Methylation in Children," *Child Development* 86, no.1 (Jan–Feb 2015): 303–09, https://doi.org/10.1111/cdev.12270.

115 Daniel Hughes and Jonathan Baylin, *Brain-Based Parenting: The Neuroscience of Caregiving for Healthy Attachment* (New York: Norton, 2012).

116 Shirtcliff et al., "Early Childhood Stress."

117 Charles A. Nelson, Nathan A. Fox, and Charles H. Zeanah, *Romania's Abandoned Children.*

118 Charles A. Nelson, Nathan A. Fox, and Charles H. Zeanah, "Anguish of the abandoned child," *Scientific American* 308, no 4 (2013): 62–67, https:doi.org/10.1038/scientificamerican0413-62.

119 Emily B. Ansell et al., "Cumulative Adversity and Smaller Gray Matter Volume in Medial Prefrontal, Anterior Cingulate, and Insula Regions," *Biological Psychiatry* 72 no.1 (2012): 57–64, https://doi.org/10.1016/j.biopsych.2011.11.022.

120 Tatiana Falcone et al., "S100B Blood Levels and Childhood Trauma in Adolescent Inpatients," *Journal of Psychiatric Research* 62 (March 2015): 14–22, http://doi.org/10.1016/j.jpsychires.2014.12.002.

121 Donna Jackson Nakazawa, *Childhood Disrupted: How Your Biography Becomes Your Biology, and How You Can Heal* (New York: Atria, 2016).

122 Nakazawa, *Childhood Disrupted*, 51.

123 "Toxic Stress," Center on the Developing Child at Harvard University. Accessed December 11, 2016, https://developingchild.harvard.edu/science/key-concepts/toxic-stress/.

124 Perry, *The Boy Who Was Raised as a Dog*, 86.

125 Nadine Burke Harris, "How Childhood Trauma Affects Health Across a Lifetime," TED video, 15:58. Posted September 2014, www.ted.com/talks/nadine_burke_harris_how_childhood_trauma_affects_health_across_a_lifetime.

126 Nakazawa, *Childhood Disrupted.*

127 Paul Tough, *Helping Children Succeed: What Works and Why* (New York, NY: Houghton Mifflin Harcourt, 2016).

128 Karl Menninger, Martin Mayman, and Paul Pruyser, *The Vital Balance: The Life Process in Mental Health* (New York: Viking Press, 1963).

129 Nicholas Hobbs, *The Troubled and Troubling Child* (San Francisco: Jossey-Bass, 1982).

130 Desmond Tutu, *No Future Without Forgiveness* (New York: Doubleday, 1999), 31.

131 Garmezy, *Children in Poverty*; Masten, *Ordinary Magic*; Werner, *Against All Odds.*

132 Roy F. Baumeiste and Mark R. Leary, "The Need to Belong: Desire for Interpersonal Attachments as a Fundamental Human Motivation," *Psychological Bulletin* 117, no. 3 (1995), 522.

133 Cozolino, *The Neuroscience of Human Relationships*, xv.

134 Bruno Bettleheim, *A Good Enough Parent: A Book on Child-Rearing* (New York: Knopf, 1988).

135 See, for example, John Bowlby, *Attachment and Loss: Volume 1* (New York: Basic Books, 1983); and Mary Ainsworth, "Attachment Beyond Infancy," *American Psychologist* 44, no. 4 (1989): 709–716.

136 Bonnie Benard, "Fostering Resilience in Children," *ERIC Digest*, August 1995, https:// files.eric.ed.gov/fulltext/ED386327.pdf; Margaret Cargo et al., "Empowerment as Fostering Positive Youth Development and Citizenship," *American Journal of Health Behavior* 27, supplement 1 (May 2003): 566–79, https://doi.org/10.5993/AJHB.27.1.s1.7; Center on the Developing Child, *The Science of Resilience*; Masten, *Ordinary Magic*; Werner, *Against All Odds.*

137 Bill Bourdon et al., "Health Initiatives for Youth: A Model of Youth/Adult Partnership Approach to HIV/AIDS Services," *Journal of Adolescent Health* 23, no. 2 (1998): 71–82, https://doi.org/10.1016/S1054-139X(98)00055-X; Lynne D. Kaltreider and Tena L. StPierre, "Beyond the Schools: Strategies for Implementing Successful Drug Prevention Programs in Community Youth-Serving Organizations," *Journal of Drug Education* 25, no. 3 (1995): 223–237, http://doi.org/10.2190/5UBA-XFJ0-1WEC-3VK3; Sehwan Kim et al., "Toward a New Paradigm in Substance Abuse and Other Problem Behavior Prevention for Youth: Youth Development and Empowerment Approach," *Journal of Drug Education* 28, no. 1 (1998): 1–17, http://doi.org/10.2190/5ET 9-X1C2-Q17B-2G6D.

138 Mary Bruce and John Bridgeland, "The Mentoring Effect: Young People's Perspectives on the Outcomes and Availability of Mentoring," Washington, DC: Civic Enterprises with Hart Research Associates for MENTOR: The National Mentoring Partnership, 2014, www.mentoring.org/images/uploads/ Report_TheMentoringEffect.pdf; Jean Rhodes et al., "Ethical Issues in Youth Mentoring," in *Handbook of Youth Mentoring*, ed. David L. DuBois and Michael J. Karcher (Thousand Oaks: Sage Publications, 2013), 511–22.

139 MENTOR: The National Mentoring Partnership, *Invest in the Future of America's Children: Support Funding for Mentoring*, 2010, http://www. mentoring.org/downloads/mentoring_1282.pdf.

140 Liesel M. Heinrich and Eleonora Gullone, "The Clinical Significance of Loneliness: A Literature Review," *Clinical Psychology Review* 16, no. 6 (2006): 695–718, https://doi.org/10.1016/j.cpr.2006.04.002.

141 Peter L. Benson, *All Kids Are Our Kids: What Communities Must Do to Raise Caring and Responsible Children and Adolescents* (San Francisco: Jossey-Bass, 2006); Katherine C. Schinka et al., "Psychosocial Predictors and Outcomes of Loneliness Trajectories from Childhood to Early Adolescence," *Journal of Adolescence* 36, no. 6 (December 2013): 1251–60, https://doi.org/10.1016/j.adolescence.2013.08.002.

142 Bronfenbrenner, "What Do Families Do?"

143 John Seita and Larry Brendtro, "Reclaiming the Unreclaimable," *Journal of Emotional and Behavioral Problems* 3, no. 4 (1995): 37–41.

144 Howard I. Bath, "Calming Together: The Pathway to Self-control," *Reclaiming Children and Youth* 16, no. 4 (2008): 44–46; Daniel J. Siegel and Mary Hartzell, *Parenting from the Inside Out: How a Deeper Self-Understanding Can Help You Raise Children Who Thrive* (Los Angeles: J. P. Tarcher, 2003).

145 Erik K. Laursen and Scott S. Birmingham, "Caring Relationships as a Protective Factor for At-Risk Youth: An Ethnographic Study," *Families in Society: The Journal of Contemporary Social Services* 84, no.2 (2003): 240–246, https://doi.org/10.1606/1044-3894.101.

146 DeAnne K. Hilfinger Messias et al., "Adult Roles in Community Programs: Implications for Best Practice," *Family Community Health* 28, no. 3 (2005): 320–37, https://0.1097/00003727-200510000-00005.

147 Eugene Roehlkepartain et al., *Relationships First: Creating Connections that Help Young People Thrive* (Minneapolis: Search Institute, 2017).

148 Junlei Li and Megan M. Julian, "Developmental Relationships as the Active Ingredient: A Unifying Working Hypothesis of 'What Works' Across Intervention Settings," *American Journal of Orthopsychiatry* 82, no. 2 (2012): 157, https://doi.org/10.1111/j.1939-0025.2012.01151.x.

149 Junlei and Julian, *Developmental Relationships as the Active Ingredient.*

150 Meghan Ellis (teacher) in discussion with author, December 2017.

151 Erik K. Laursen, "The Healing Power of Jazz and Relationships" (October 2013), https://www.starr.org/research/healing-power-jazz-and-relationships.

152 René Veenstra et al., "Network-Behavior Dynamics," *Journal of Research on Adolescence* 23, no. 3 (2013): 399–412. https://doi.org/10.1111/jora.12070.

153 Alicia D. Lynch et al., "Adolescent Academic Achievement and School Engagement: An Examination of the Role of School-Wide Peer Culture," *Journal of Youth and Adolescence* 42, no.1 (2013): 6–19, https://doi.org/10.1007/s10964-012-9833-0.

154 Thomas J. Dishion et al., "When Interventions Harm. Peer Groups and Problem Behavior," *American Psychologist* 54, no 9 (1999): 755–64, https://doi.org/10.1037/0003-066X.54.9.755.

155 Kenneth A. Dodge et al., "Deviant Peer Influences in Intervention and Public Policy for Youth," *Society for Research in Child Development Social Policy Report*

20, no 1. (2006): 3–19, https://files.eric.ed.gov/fulltext/ED521749.pdf; Lynch, "Adolescent Academic Achievement and School Engagement."

156 Centers for Disease Control and Prevention, *School Connectedness: Strategies for Increasing Protective Factors Among Youth* (Atlanta: US Department of Health and Human Services, 2009), 3.

157 Centers for Disease Control and Prevention, *School Connectedness.*

158 Erik Schapps, "The Role of Supportive School Environments in Promoting Academic Success," in *Getting Results, Developing Safe and Healthy Kids Update: Student Health, Supportive Schools, and Academic Success*, 17–52. Developed by the Safe and Healthy Kids Program Office, California Department of Education, 2005, http://cscd.rutgers.edu/file/getresults5_ch3Schaps.pdf; Dorian Wilson, "The Interface of School Climate and School Connectedness and Relationships with Aggression and Victimization," *Journal of School Health* 74, no. 7 (2004): 293–99, https://doi.org/10.1111/j.1746-1561.2004.tb08286.x.

159 Centers for Disease Control and Prevention, *Fostering School Connectedness. Information for Teachers* (July 2009), 1, https://www.cdc.gov/healthyyouth/protective/pdf/connectedness_teachers.pdf.

160 Heather S. Lonczak et al., "Effects of the Seattle Social Development Project: Behavior, Pregnancy, Birth, and Sexually Transmitted Disease Outcomes by Age 21," *Archives of Pediatric Adolescent Health* 156, no. 5 (2002): 438–47, https://doi.org/10.1001/archpedi.156.5.438; Oddrun Samdal et al., "Achieving Health and Educational Goals Through Schools—A Study of the Importance of the School Climate and the Students' Satisfaction with School," *Health Education Research* 13, no. 3 (September 1998): 383–97, https://doi.org/10.1093/her/13.3.383.

161 James Patrick Connell et al., "Hanging in There: Behavioral, Psychological, and Contextual Factors Affecting Whether African-American Adolescents Stay in School," *Journal of Adolescent Research* 10, no 1 (1995): 41–63, https://doi.org/10.1177/0743554895101004; Adena M. Klem and James P. Connel, "Relationships Matter: Linking Teacher Support to Student Engagement and Achievement," *Journal of School Health* 74, no. 7 (2004): 262–273, https://doi.org/10.1111/j.1746-1561.2004.tb08283.x; Kathryn R. Wentzel, "Social Relationships and Motivation in Middle School," *Journal of Educational Psychology* 90, no. 2 (1998): 202–209, https://doi.org/10.1037/0022-0663.90.2.202.

162 Erik K. Laursen, "Rather than Fixing Kids: Build Positive Peer Cultures," *Reclaiming Children and Youth* 14, no. 3 (Fall 2005): 137–42.

163 Erik K. Laursen and Thomas F. Tate, "Democratic Group Work," *Reclaiming Children and Youth* 20, no. 4 (Winter 2012): 46–51.

164 Erik K. Laursen, "Positive Peer Cultures and the Developing Brain," *Reclaiming Children and Youth* 18, no.2 (Spring 2009): 8–11.

165 “Class Meetings: Creating a Safe School Starting in Your Classroom,” The Ophelia Project (2013). Accessed from http://www.opheliaproject.org/cass/ClassMeetings.pdf; Riese M. Snyder et al., *Class meetings that Matter: A Year's Worth of Resources for Grades 9-12* (Center City, MN: Hazelden, 2012), accessed from https://www.hazelden.org/HAZ_MEDIA/3981_ClassMeetingsThatMatter.pdf.

166 Jamie Leech (teacher) in discussion with author, December 2017.

167 Tom Rath and Mary Reckmeyer, *How Full Is Your Bucket? For Kids* (New York: Gallup Press, 2009).

168 Neal Sarahan (codirector) in discussion with author, December 2017.

169 *Chad*, Changing Minds, YouTube video, 5:42 Posted May 8, 2017, https://www.youtube.com/watch?v=MTp2MZaFDvk.

170 EdVisions Design Essentials, “Positive, Caring Relationships; Respect and Responsibility Modeled and Practiced.” You Tube video, 6:52. Posted January 7, 2011. https://www.youtube.com/watch?v=P3gg4dvAR1g

171 Rita R. Pierson, “Every Kid Needs a Champion,” TED video, 7:45. Posted May 2013, https://www.ted.com/talks/rita_pierson_every_kid_needs_a_champion.

172 Search Institute, “The Power of Relationships in the Lives of Youth,” YouTube video, 4:06. Posted August 5, 2017. https://www.youtube.com/watch?v=NPW3ko6GoNE.

173 American Psychiatric Association, *Diagnostic and Statistical Manual of Mental Disorders* (Arlington: American Psychiatric Association, 2013).

174 VIA Institute on Character, *VIA Survey*, accessed January 5, 2018, https://www.viacharacter.org/survey/account/register

175 Ryan M. Niemiec, *Character Strengths Interventions: A Field Guide for Practitioners* (Ashland: Hogrefe, 2017), 17.

176 Niemiec, *Character Strengths Interventions,* 17.

177 Al Desetta and Sybil Wolin, *The Struggle to be Strong: True Stories by Teens About Overcoming Tough Times* (Minneapolis: Free Spirit Publishing, 2000).

178 Steven Wolin and Sybil Wolin, *Survivor's Pride: Introduction to Resiliency* [DVD] (United States: Attainment Company, 2012).

179 Peterson, *Character Strengths and Virtues.*

180 Niemiec, *Character Strengths Interventions.*

181 Ryan M. Niemiec, *Session 5: A working model* [Class handout] (VIA intensive Online, The activation of strengths: Bridging research on character strengths into practice: May–June 2011); Niemiec. *Character Strengths Interventions.*

182 Wolin, *Survivor's Pride.*

183 Niemiec, *Character Strengths Interventions.*

184 Ryan Niemiec, “How to Identify VIA Character Strengths: Strength Spotting,” last updated June 26, 2013, http://www.viacharacter.org/blog/how-to-identif y-via-character-strengths-to-bring-out-the-best-in-others/.

185 VIA Institute on Character, "VIA PRO Character Strengths Profile," accessed January 3, 2018, https://www.viacharacter.org/www/Portals/0/VIA percent20Pro percent20Report.pdf.

186 Tayyab Rashid and Afroze Anjum, "340 Ways to Use VIA Character Strengths" (2011), accessed February 8, 2017, https://www.scribd.com/document/312008980/340-Ways-to-Use-Strengths-Tayyab-Rashid.

187 Seligman, *Flourish.*

188 Michelle McQuaide, "VIA Strengths Mural," Featured Resources (October 16, 2014), http://www.viacharacter.org/resources/via-strengths-mural/.

189 Kasia Borkowski (teacher) in discussion with author, January 2018.

190 Wade Puryear (vice president of education) in discussion with author, March 2017.

191 Ryan Niemiec, "A Universal Language that Describes What's Best in Us," YouTube video, 18:58. Posted June 17, 2017, https://www.youtube.com/watch?v=DMWck0mKGWc.

192 Niemic, *Character Strengths Interventions.*

193 Ryan M. Niemiec, *Mindfulness and Character Strengths: A Practical Guide to Flourishing* (Ashland: Hogrefe, 2014).

194 Shannon Polly, and Kathryn B. Britton, *Character Strengths Matter. How to Live a Full Life* (Positive Psychology News, 2015), Kindle.

195 Center on the Developing Child at Harvard University, "Executive Functions and Self-Regulation," accessed December 11, 2016, https://developingchild.harvard.edu/science/key-concepts/executive -function/.

196 Tracy Packiam Alloway and Ross G. Alloway, "Investigating the Predictive Roles of Working Memory and IQ in Academic Attainment," *Journal of Experimental Child Psychology* 106 (2010): 20–29, https://doi.org/10.1016/j.jecp.2009.11.003.

197 Russel A. Barkley, *Executive Functions: What They Are, How They Work, and Why They Evolved* (New York: Guilford Press, 2012).

198 Center on the Developing Child at Harvard University, "Enhancing and Practicing Executive Function Skills with Children from Infancy to Adolescence," PDF, 2014, http://www.developingchild.harvard.edu.

199 Craig Simmons (licensed professional counselor) in discussion with author, March 2016.

200 Gioia, *Rating Inventory of Executive Function.*

201 Adapted from Gioia, *Rating Inventory of Executive Function.*

202 Center on the Developing Child, "Enhancing and Practicing Executive Function Skills."

203 Sheri Wilkins and Carol Burmeister, *FLIPP the Switch: Strengthen Executive Function Skills* (Lenaxa: Autism Asperger Publishing, 2015).

204 Barbara Rogoff, *Developing Destinies. A Mayan Midwife and Town* (New York, NY: Oxford, 2011): 17–18, Kindle.

205 National Scientific Council on the Developing Child, *Supportive Relationships and Active Skill-Building*; Ashley B. Evans et al., "Racial Socialization as a Mechanism for Positive Development Among African American Youth," *Child Development Perspectives* 6, no. 3 (2012): 251–257, http://doi.org/10.1111/j.1750-8606.2011.00226.x; Lawrence J. Kirmayer et al., "Rethinking Resilience from Indigenous Perspectives," *The Canadian Journal of Psychiatry* 56, no. 2 (2011): 84–91, https://doi.org/10.1177/070674371105600203.

206 Zaretta L. Hammond, *Culturally Responsive Teaching and the Brain: Promoting Authentic Engagement and Rigor Among Culturally and Linguistically Diverse Students* (Thousand Oaks: Corwin, 2015).

207 Rogoff, *Developing Destinies*, 15.

208 Soong-Chan Rah, *Many Colors: Cultural Intelligence for a Changing Church* (Chicago: Moody Publishers, 2010), Kindle.

209 Adapted from Rah, *Many Colors.*

210 Geert Hofstede, *Culture's Consequences: Comparing Values, Behaviors, Institutions and Organizations Across Nations* (New York: Black Classic Press, 2001); Geert Hofstede et al., *Cultures and Organizations: Software of the Mind* (New York: McGraw-Hill, 2010).

211 The Six Dimensions of National Culture, Hofstede Insights, accessed November 3, 2016, https://www.hofstede-insights.com/models/national-culture/.

212 Dianne Wepa, "Culture and Ethnicity: What is the Question?" in *Cultural Safety in Aotearoa New Zealand*, ed. Dianne Wepa (Port Melbourne, Australia: Cambridge University Press), 65–78.

213 Tricia Giles-Wang, health and well-being consultant for First Nations, Metís, and Inuit education, in discussion with author, January 2018.

214 Gregg Morris, lead educator and creator at Mahana Culture, in discussion with author, January 2018.

215 Hammond, *Culturally Responsive Teaching.*

216 Rah, *Many Colors.*

217 Peter R. Breggin, *The Art of Being Helpful* (New York: Springer, 1997), 7.

218 Colm O'Riordan, "A Forgiving Strategy for the Iterated Prisoner's Dilemma," *Journal of Artificial Societies and Social Simulation* 3, no. 4 (2000), http://jasss.soc.surrey.ac.uk/3/4/3.html; William H. Press and Freeman J. Dyson, "Iterated Prisoner's Dilemma Contains Strategies that Dominate any Evolutionary Opponent," *Proceedings of the National Academy of Sciences* 109, no. 26 (2012): 10409-13, https://doi.org/10.1073/pnas.1206569109.

219 Bronfenbrenner, *American Values*, 2.

220 Thomas Lewis et al., *A General Theory of Love* (New York: Vintage/Random House, 2000), 86.

221 Allan Schore, as quoted by Benedict Carey, "Shaping the Connection: Studies Renew Interest in Effects of the Parent-Child Bond," *Los Angeles Times*, March 31, 2003, paragraph 16, http://articles.latimes.com/2003/mar/31/health/he-attachment31.

222 Louis Cozolino, *The Neuroscience of Human Relationships: Attachment and the Developing Social Brain* (New York: Norton, 2006), 14.

223 Jack P. Shonkoff and Deborah A. Phillips, *From Neurons to Neighborhoods: The Science of Early Childhood Development* (Washington, DC: National Academic Press, 2000).

224 Gordon Neufeld and Gabor Maté, *Hold on to Your Kids: Why Parents Need to Matter More Than Peers* (New York: Ballantine Books, 2014).

225 Cozolino, *Neuroscience of Human Relationships;* Barry L. Duncan et al., *The Heart & Soul of Change: Delivering What Works in Therapy* (Washington, DC: American Psychological Association, 2010); Stephanie Mihalas et al., "Cultivating Caring Relationships Between Teachers and Secondary Students with Emotional and Behavioral Disorders: Implications for Research and Practice," *Remedial and Special Education* 30, no.2 (2008): 108–25, https://doi.org/10.1177/0741932508315950.

226 Stephen W. Porges, *The Polyvagal Theory: Neurophysiological Foundation of Emotions, Attachment, Communication, and Self-Regulation* (New York: Norton, 2011).

227 Mark D. Freado et al., "The Inside Kid: A Little Light in a Dark, Dark Night," *Reclaiming Children and Youth* 12, no. 4 (2004): 194–198.

228 Jamie C. Chambers and Mark Freado, *The Art of Kid Whispering: Reclaiming the Inside Kid* (CreateSpace Independent Publishing Platform, 2015).

229 Siegel and Hartwell, *Parenting from the Inside Out.*

230 Robert Fuller, *Somebodies and Nobodies: Overcoming the Abuse of Rank* (Gabriola Island: New Society Publishers, 2003).

231 Rachel Vernon and Elaine Papps, "Cultural Safety and Continuing Competence," in *Cultural Safety in Aotearoa New Zealand*, ed. Dianne Wepa (Port Melbourne: Cambridge University, 2015), 51–64.

232 Bernadette von Dawans et al., "The Social Dimension of Stress Reactivity: Acute Stress Increases Prosocial Behavior in Humans," *Psychological Science* 23, no. 7 (2012): 651–60, https://doi.org/10.1177/0956797611431576.

233 Allison Clark and June Statham, "Listening to Young Children: Experts in Their Own Lives," *Adoption and Fostering* 29, no. 1 (2005): 45–56, https://doi.org/10.1177/030857590502900106.

234 Hammond, *Culturally Responsive Teaching.*

235 Michael White and David Epston, *Narrative Ways to Therapeutic Ends* (New York: Norton, 1990).

236 Michael White, "The externalization of the problem and the re-authoring of lives and relationships," *Dulwich Centre Newsletter* (1969): 3–21.

237 White and Epston, *Narrative Ways.*

238 Steve de Shazer, *More than Miracles.*

239 See Milton H. Erickson, "Pseudo-Orientation in Time as an Hypnotherapeutic Procedure," *Journal of Clinical and Experimental Hypnosis* 2, no. 4 (1954): 261–283, http://doi.org/10.1080/00207145408410117; and Steve de Shazer, *Clues: Investigating Solutions in Brief Therapy* (New York: Norton, 1988), 5.

240 Bannink, *Post Traumatic Stress*, 15.

241 Roger E. Allen and Stephen D. Allen, *Winnie-the-Pooh on Success* (New York: Dutton, 1997), 17.

242 Angela Duckworth, *Grit: The Power of Perseverance and Passion* (New York: HarperCollins, 2016).

243 US Department of Education, *Promoting Grit, Tenacity, and Perseverance: Critical Factors in the 21st Century* (US Department of Education, Office of Educational Technology: February 2013), 15, http://pgbovine.net/OET-Draft-Grit-Report-2-17-13.pdf.

244 Jennifer Martin and Carol Stuart, "Working with Cyberspace in the Life-space," *Relational Child and Youth Care Practice* 24, no. 1–2 (2011): 55–66.

245 Harvey Ratner and Denise Yusuf, *Brief Counselling with Children and Young People* (New York: Routledge, 2015).

246 Matthew D. Selekman, *Pathways to Change: Brief Therapy Solutions with Difficult Adolescents* (New York, NY: The Guilford Press, 1993).

Bibliography

Ainsworth, Mary. "Attachment Beyond Infancy." *American Psychologist* 44, no. 4 (1989): 709–716.

Allen, Roger E., and Stephen D. Allen. *Winnie-the-Pooh on Success.* New York: Dutton, 1997.

Alloway, Tracy Packiam, and Ross G. Alloway. "Investigating the Predictive Roles of Working Memory and IQ in Academic Attainment." *Journal of Experimental Child Psychology* 106, (2010): 20–29. https://doi.org/10.1016/j.jecp.2009.11.003.

American Academy of Pediatrics. "Adverse Childhood Experiences and Lifelong Consequences of Trauma" (2014). https://www.aap.org/en-us/Documents/ttb_aces_consequences.pdf.

American Psychiatric Association. *Diagnostic and Statistical Manual of Mental Disorders.* Arlington: American Psychiatric Association, 2013.

Anda, Robert F., and Vincent J. Felitti. "Adverse Childhood Experiences and Their Relationship to Adult Well-Being and Disease: Turning Gold into Lead," last modified August 27, 2012. https://www.thenationalcouncil.org/wp-content/uploads/2012/11/Natl-Council-Webinar-8-2012.pdf.

Anglin, James P. *Pain, Normality and the Struggle for Congruence: Reinterpreting Residential Care for Children and Youth.* New York: Haworth Press, 2002.

Angyal, Andras. *Neurosis and Treatment: A Holistic Theory.* Edited by Eugenia Hanfmann and Richard M. Jones. New York: J. Wiley, 1965.

Ansell, Emily B., Kenneth Rando, Keri Tuit, Joseph Guarnaccia, and Rajita Sinha. "Cumulative Adversity and Smaller Gray Matter Volume in Medial Prefrontal, Anterior Cingulate, and Insula Regions." *Biological Psychiatry* 72, no.1 (2012): 57–64. https://doi.org/10.1016/j.biopsych.2011.11.022.

Baker, Paul W., and Meredith White-McMahon. *The Hopeful Brain: NeuroRelational Repair for Disconnected Children and Youth.* Lulu Publishing Services, 2014.

Bandura, Albert. "Exercise of personal and collective efficacy in changing societies." In *Self-efficacy and Changing Societies,* edited by Albert Bandura, 1–44. New York: Cambridge University Press, 1995.

Bannink, Fredrike. *Post Traumatic Success: Positive Psychology and Solution-Focused Strategies to Help Clients Survive and Thrive.* New York: W. W. Norton, 2014.

Barkley, Russel A. *Executive Functions: What They Are, How They Work, and Why They Evolved.* New York: Guilford Press, 2012.

Bath, Howard I. "Calming Together: The Pathway to Self-control." *Reclaiming Children and Youth* 16, no. 4 (2008): 44–46.

Baumeister, Roy F., and Mark R. Leary. "The Need to Belong: Desire for Interpersonal Attachments as a Fundamental Human Motivation." *Psychological Bulletin* 117, no. 3 (1995): 497–529.

Beah, Ishmael. *A Long Way Gone: Memoirs of a Boy Soldier.* New York: Sarah Crichton Books, 2007.

Benard, Bonnie. "Fostering Resilience in Children." ERIC Digest, August 1995. https:// files.eric.ed.gov/fulltext/ED386327.pdf.

Benson, Peter L. *All Kids Are Our Kids: What Communities Must Do to Raise Caring and Responsible Children and Adolescents.* San Francisco: Jossey-Bass, 2006.

Bettleheim, Bruno. *A Good Enough Parent: A Book on Child-Rearing.* New York: Knopf, 1988.

Bourdon, Bill, Steven Tierney, G. J. Huba, Joanne Lothrop, Lisa A. Melchior, Ruth Betru, and Kim Compoc. "Health Initiatives for Youth: A Model of Youth/Adult Partnership Approach to HIV/AIDS Services." *Journal of Adolescent Health* 23, no. 2 (1998): 71–82. https://doi.org/10.1016/S1054-139X(98)00055-X.

Bowlby, John. *Attachment and Loss: Volume 1.* New York: Basic Books, 1983.

Breggin, Peter R. *The Art of Being Helpful.* New York: Springer, 1997.

Brendtro, Larry K., and Leslie D. du Toit. *Response Ability Pathways: Restoring Bonds of Respect.* Cape Town: Pretext, 2005.

Brendtro, Larry K., and Martin L. Mitchell. *Deep Brain Learning: Evidence-based Essentials in Education, Treatment, and Youth Development.* Albion: Circle of Courage/Starr Commonwealth, 2015.

Brendtro, Larry K., Martin Brokenleg, and Steve van Bockern. *Reclaiming Youth at Risk: Our Hope for the Future.* Bloomington: Solution Tree, 2002.

Bronfenbrenner, Urie. "What Do Families Do?" *Institute for American Values* 2 (Winter/Spring, 1991).

Brooks, Robert, and Sam Goldstein. *Raising Resilient Children: Fostering Strength, Hope, and Optimism in Your Child.* Chicago: Contemporary Books, 2001.

Brown, Waln K., and John Seita. *Growing up in the Care of Strangers: The Experiences, Insights and Recommendations of Eleven Former Foster Kids.* Tallahassee: William Gladden Foundation Press, 2009.

Bruce, Mary, and John Bridgeland. *The Mentoring Effect: Young People's Perspectives on the Outcomes and Availability of Mentoring.* Washington, DC: Civic Enterprises with Hart Research Associates for MENTOR: The National Mentoring Partnership, 2014. www.mentoring.org/images/uploads/Report_TheMentoringEffect.pdf.

Bucci, Monica, Lisa Gutiérrez Wang, Kadiatou Koita, Sukhdip Purewal, Sara Silvério Marques, Nadine Burke Harris. *Center for Youth Wellness ACE-Questionnaire User Guide.* San Francisco, CA: Center for Youth Wellness, 2015.

Burke Harris, Nadine, and T. Renschler. *Center for Youth Wellness ACE-Questionnaire.* San Francisco: Center for Youth Wellness, 2015.

Burke Harris, Nadine. "How Childhood Trauma Affects Health Across a Lifetime." TED video, 15:58. Posted September 2014. www.ted.com/talks/nadine_burke_harris_how_childhood_trauma_affects_health_across_a_lifetime.

Calcaterra, Regina. *Etched in Sand: A True Story of Five Siblings Who Survived an Unspeakable Childhood on Long Island.* New York: William Morrow, 2013.

Carey, Benedict. "Shaping the Connection: Studies Renew Interest in Effects of the Parent-Child Bond." *Los Angeles Times* (March 31, 2003), paragraph 16. http://articles.latimes.com/2003/mar/31/health/he-attachment31.

Cargo, Margaret., Garry D. Grams, Judith M. Ottoson, Patricia Ward, and Lawrence W. Green. "Empowerment as Fostering Positive Youth Development and Citizenship." *American Journal of Health Behavior* 27, Supplement 1 (May 2003): 566–79. https://doi.org/10.5993/AJHB.27.1.s1.7.

Carson, Clayborne, and Peter Holloran, eds. *A Knock at Midnight: Inspiration from the Great Sermons of Reverend Martin Luther King, Jr.* New York: Warner Books, 2000.

Center on the Developing Child at Harvard University. "Experiences Build Brain Architecture." YouTube video, 1:56. Posted September 29, 2011. https://www.youtube.com/watch?v=VNNsN9IJkws.

Center on the Developing Child at Harvard University. "Serve and Return Shape Brain Circuitry." YouTube video, 1:42. Posted September 29, 2011. https://www.youtube.com/watch?v=m_5u8-QSh6A.

Center on the Developing Child at Harvard University. "Enhancing and Practicing Executive Function Skills with Children from Infancy to Adolescence." PDF, 2014. http://www.developingchild.harvard.edu.

Center on the Developing Child at Harvard University. *The Science of Resilience.* In Brief, 2015. https://46y5eh11fhgw3ve3ytpwxt9r-wpengine.netdna-ssl.com/wp-content/uploads/2015/05/InBrief-The-Science-of-Resilience.pdf.

Center on the Developing Child at Harvard University. "From Best Practices to Breakthrough Impacts: A Science-based Approach to Building a More Promising Future for Young Children and Families." PDF, 2016. http://www.developingchild.harvard.edu.

Center on the Developing Child at Harvard University. "Toxic Stress." Accessed December 11, 2016. https://developingchild.harvard.edu/science/key-concepts/toxic-stress/.

Center on the Developing Child at Harvard University. "Executive Functions and Self-Regulation." Accessed December 11, 2016. https://developingchild.harvard.edu/science/key-concepts/executive -function/.

Centers for Disease Control and Prevention. *Fostering School Connectedness. Information for Teachers.* July 2009. https://www.cdc.gov/healthyyouth/protective/pdf/connectedness_teachers.pdf.

Centers for Disease Control and Prevention. *School Connectedness. Information for School Districts and School Administrators.* July 2009. https://www.cdc.gov/healthyyouth/protective/pdf/connectedness_administrators.pdf

Centers for Disease Control and Prevention. *School Connectedness: Strategies for Increasing Protective Factors Among Youth.* Atlanta: U.S. Department of Health and Human Services, 2009.

Chad. Changing Minds. You Tube video, 5:42 Posted May 8, 2017. https://www.youtube.com/watch?v=MTp2MZaFDvk

Chambers, Jamie, C., and Mark Freado. *The Art of Kid Whispering: Reclaiming the Inside Kid.* CreateSpace Independent Publishing Platform, 2015.

Child Trends Bank. *Adverse Experiences: Indicators on Children and Youth.* July 2013. http://www.childtrends.org/wp-content/uploads/2013/07/124_Adverse_Experiences.pdf

Children's Bureau. *The AFCARS Report. Preliminary FY 2014 Estimates as of July 2015. No. 22.* U.S. Department of Health and Human Services, Administration for Children and Families, Administration on Children, Youth and Families. Washington, D.C. July 2015. http://www.acf.hhs.gov/sites/default/files/cb/afcarsreport22.pdf

Clark, Allison, and June Statham (2005). "Listening to Young Children: Experts in Their Own Lives." *Adoption and Fostering* 29, no. 1 (2005): 45-56. https://doi.org/10.1177/030857590502900106

Connell, James Patrick, Bonnie L. Halpern-Felsher, Elisabeth Clifford, Warren Crichlow, and Peter Usinger. "Hanging in There: Behavioral, Psychological, and Contextual Factors

Affecting Whether African-American Adolescents Stay in School." *Journal of Adolescent Research* 10, no 1 (1995): 41–63. https://doi.org/10.1177/0743554895101004

Cozolino, Louis. *The Neuroscience of Human Relationships: Attachment and the Developing Social Brain.* New York: Norton, 2006.

Cozolino, Louis. *The Neuroscience of Education: Optimizing Attachment & Learning in the Classroom.* New York: Norton, 2013.

Cozolino, Louis. *The Neuroscience of Human Relationships: Attachment and the Developing Social Brain.* 2nd ed. New York: Norton, 2014.

Craig, Susan. *Reaching and Teaching Children Who Hurt: Strategies for Your Classroom.* East Peoria: Brookes Publishing, 2008.

Csikszentmihalyi, Mihaly. *Flow: The Psychology of Optimal Experience.* New York: HarperCollins, 1990.

Csikszentmihalyi, Mihaly. *Finding Flow: The Psychology of Engagement with Everyday Life.* New York, NY: Basic Books, 1990.

Data Resource Center for Child and Adolescent Health. *2016 National Survey of Children's Health.* Accessed February 14, 2017 from http://www.childhealthdata.org/learn/NSCH.

de Shazer, Steve. *Clues: Investigating Solutions in Brief Therapy.* New York: Norton, 1988.

de Shazer, Steve, and Yvonne M. Dolan. *More than Miracles: The State of the Art of Solution-Focused Brief Therapy.* New York: Haworth Press, 2007.

Desetta, Al, and Sybil Wolin. *The Struggle to be Strong: True Stories by Teens about Overcoming Tough Times.* Minneapolis: Free Spirit Publishing, 2000.

Dishion, Thomas J., Joan McCord, and Francois Poulin. "When Interventions Harm. Peer Groups and Problem Behavior." *American Psychologist* 54, no 9 (1999): 755–64. https://doi.org/10.1037/0003-066X.54.9.755.

Dodge, Kenneth A., Thomas J. Dishion, and Jennifer E. Lansford. "Deviant Peer Influences in Intervention and Public Policy for Youth." *Society for Research in Child Development Social Policy Report* 20, no 1 (2006): 3–19. https://files.eric.ed.gov/fulltext/ED521749.pdf.

Dolan, M., C. Casanueva, K. Smith, and H. Ringeisen. *NSCAW child well-being spotlight: More Than One Quarter of Children Placed Out of Home Experience Placement Disruption in the First 18 Months After a Maltreatment Investigation.* OPRE report #2013-05. (Washington, DC: Office of Planning, Research and Evaluation, Administration for Children and Families, U.S. Department of Health and Human Services, February 2013).

Duncan, Barry L., Scott D. Miller, Bruce E. Wampold, and Mark A. Hubble. *The Heart & Soul of Change: Delivering What Works in Therapy.* Washington, DC: American Psychological Association, 2010.

Duckworth, Angela. *Grit: The Power of Perseverance and Passion.* New York: HarperCollins, 2016.

EdVisions Design Essentials. "Positive, Caring Relationships; Respect and Responsibility Modeled and Practiced." YouTube video, 6:52. Posted January 7, 2011. https://www.youtube.com/watch?v=P3gg4dvAR1g.

Eiseley, Loren. *The Star Thrower.* New York: Harvest Books, 1979.

Ellis, Wendy R., and William H. Dietz. "A New Framework for Addressing Adverse Childhood and Community Experiences: The Building Community Resilience Model." *Academic Pediatrics* 17, no. 7 (October 2017): S86–S93. https:/doi.org/10.1016/j.acap.2016.12.011.

Erickson, Milton H. "Pseudo-Orientation in Time as an Hypnotherapeutic Procedure." *Journal of Clinical and Experimental Hypnosis* 2, no. 4 (1954): 261–283. http://doi.org/10.1080/00207145408410117.

Evans, Ashley B., Meeta Banerjee, Rika Meyer, Adriana Aldana, Monica Foust, and Stephanie Rowley. "Racial Socialization as a Mechanism for Positive Development Among African American Youth." *Child Development Perspectives* 6, no. 3 (2012): 251–257. http://doi.org/10.1111/j.1750-8606.2011.00226.x.

Falcone, Tatiana, Damir Janigro, Rachel Lovell, Barry Simon, Charles A. Brown, Mariela Herrera, Aye Nu Myint, and Amit Anad. "S100B Blood Levels and Childhood Trauma in Adolescent Inpatients." *Journal of Psychiatric Research* 62 (March 2015): 14–22. http://doi.org/10.1016/j.jpsychires.2014.12.002.

Felitti, Vincent J., Robert F. Anda, Dale Nordenberg, David F. Williamson, Allison M. Spitz, Valerie Edwards, Mary P. Koss, and James S. Marks. "Relationship of Childhood Abuse and Household Dysfunction to Many of the Leading Causes of Death in Adults." *American Journal of Preventive Medicine* 14, no. 4 (1998): 245–258. http://doi.org/10.1016/s0749-3797(98)00017-8.

Fisher, Antwone Q., and Mim E. Rivas. *Finding Fish: A Memoir.* New York: Morrow, 2001.

Freado, Mark D., Jeffrey W. McCombie, and Dennis Bussel. "The Inside Kid: A Little Light in a Dark, Dark Night." *Reclaiming Children and Youth* 12, no. 4 (2004): 194–198.

Fuller, Robert. *Somebodies and Nobodies: Overcoming the Abuse of Rank.* Gabriola Island: New Society Publishers, 2003.

Gable, Shelly L., and Jonathan Haidt. "What (and Why) is Positive Psychology?" *Review of General Psychology* 9, no. 2 (2005): 103–110. http://doi.org/10.1037/1089-2680.9.2.103.

Garmezy, Norman. "Children in Poverty: Resilience Despite Risk." *Psychiatry* 56, no. 1 (1993): 127–136. https://doi.org/10.1080/00332747.1993.11024627.

Gioia, Gerard A., Peter K. Isquith, Steven C. Guy, and Lauren Kenworthy. *Rating Inventory of Executive Function.* Lutz: PAR, 2016.

Goleman, Daniel. *Emotional Intelligence: Why It Matters More Than IQ.* New York: Bantam Books, 1995.

Hammond, Zaretta L. *Culturally Responsive Teaching and the Brain: Promoting Authentic Engagement and Rigor Among Culturally and Linguistically Diverse Students.* Thousand Oaks: Corwin, 2015.

Harvard Health Publications. "Understanding the Stress Response: Chronic Activation of This Survival Mechanism Impairs Health." Last updated March 18, 2016. http://www.health.harvard.edu/staying-healthy/understanding-the-stress-response.

Heinrich, Liesl M., and Eleonora Gullone. "The Clinical Significance of Loneliness: A Literature Review." *Clinical Psychology Review* 16, no. 6 (2006): 695–718. https://doi.org/10.1016/j.cpr.2006.04.002.

Hill, Patrick L., and Nicholas A. Turiano. "Purpose in Life as Predictor of Mortality across Adulthood." *Psychological Science* 25, no. 7 (May 2014): 1482–86. https://doi.org/10.1177/0956797614531799.

Hobbs, Nicholas. *The Troubled and Troubling Child.* San Francisco: Jossey-Bass, 1982.

Hoffman, Martin L. "Is Altruism Part of Human Nature?" *Journal of Personality and Social Psychology* 40, no. 1 (1981): 121–137. http://dx.doi.org/10.1037/0022-3514.40.1.121.

Hoffman, Martin L. "Is Altruism Part of Human Nature?" *Journal of Personality and Social Psychology* 40, no. 1 (1981): 121–137.

Hofstede, Geert. *Culture's Consequences: Comparing Values, Behaviors, Institutions and Organizations across Nations.* New York: Black Classic Press, 2001.

Hofstede, Geert, Gert Jan Hofstede, and Michael Minkov. *Cultures and Organizations. Software of the Mind.* New York: McGraw-Hill, 2010.

Hughes, Daniel, and Jonathan Baylin. *Brain-Based Parenting: The Neuroscience of Caregiving for Healthy Attachment.* New York: Norton, 2012.

International Positive Psychology Association. Accessed August 12, 2016. http://www.ippanetwork.org.

James, Susan Donaldson. "Homeless to Harvard: Child of Addicts Counsels Youth in Spirituality." *ABC News*, October 10, 2013. http://abcnews.go.com/Health/homeless-harvard-child-addicts-counsels-youth-spirituality/story?id=20523916.

Jensen, Frances E., and Amy Ellis Nutt. *The Teenage Brain: A Neuroscientist's Survival Guide to Raising Adolescents and Young Adults.* New York: HarperCollins, 2015.

Kaltreider Lynne D., and Tena L. StPierre. "Beyond the Schools: Strategies for Implementing Successful Drug Prevention Programs in Community Youth-Serving Organizations." *Journal of Drug Education* 25, no. 3 (1995): 223–237. http://doi.org/10.2190/5UBA-XFJ0-1WEC-3VK3.

Kim, Sehwan, Charles Crutchfield, Charles Williams, and Nancy Hepler. "Toward a New Paradigm in Substance Abuse and Other Problem Behavior Prevention for Youth: Youth Development and Empowerment Approach." *Journal of Drug Education* 28, no. 1 (1998): 1–17. http://doi.org/10.2190/5ET9-X1C2-Q17B-2G6D.

Kirmayer, Lawrence J., Stephanie Dandeneau, Elisabeth Marshall, Morgan Kahentonni Phillips, and Karla Jessen Williamson.

"Rethinking Resilience from Indigenous Perspectives." *The Canadian Journal of Psychiatry* 56, no. 2 (2011): 84–91. https://doi.org/10.1177/070674371105600203.

Klem, Adena M., and James P. Connel. "Relationships Matter: Linking Teacher Support to Student Engagement and Achievement." *Journal of School Health* 74, no. 7 (2004): 262–273. https://doi.org/10.1111/j.1746-1561.2004.tb08283.x.

Koltko-Rivera, Mark E. "Rediscovering the Later Version of Maslow's Hierarchy of Needs: Self-Transcendence and Opportunities for Theory, Research, and Unification." *Review of General Psychology* 10, no. 4 (2006): 302–317. https://dor.org/10.1037/1089-2680.10.4.302.

Kriete, Roxanne, and Carol Davis. *The Morning Meeting Book.* Turner Falls: Center for Responsive Schools, 2014.

Laursen, Erik K. "Seven Habits of Reclaiming Relationships." *Reclaiming Children and Youth* 11, no. 1 (Spring 2002): 1–14.

Laursen, Erik K. "Strength-Based Practice with Children in Trouble." *Reclaiming Children and Youth* 9, no. 2 (Spring 2002): 70–75.

Laursen, Erik K. "Rather than Fixing Kids: Build Positive Peer Cultures." *Reclaiming Children and Youth* 14, no. 3 (Fall 2005): 137-42.

Laursen, Erik K. "Positive Peer Cultures and the Developing Brain." *Reclaiming Children and Youth* 18, no.2 (Spring 2009): 8–11.

Laursen, Erik K. "The Healing Power of Jazz and Relationships." (October 2013). https://www.starr.org/research/healing-power-jazz-and-relationships.

Laursen, Erik K. "Intentional Collisions: Kindling Connections." *Reclaiming Children and* Youth 24, no. 2 (Spring 2015): 27–32.

Laursen, Erik, and Scott S. Birmingham. "Caring Relationships as a Protective Factor for At-Risk Youth: An Ethnographic Study." *Families in Society: The Journal of Contemporary Social Services* 84, no.2 (2003): 240–246. https://doi.org/10.1606/1044-3894.101.

Laursen, Erik K., and Thomas F. Tate. "Democratic Group Work." *Reclaiming Children and Youth* 20, no. 4 (Winter 2012): 46–51.

Lerner, Richard M. *The Good Teen: Rescuing Adolescence from the Myth of the Storm and Stress Years.* New York: Crown, 2007.

Lewis, Thomas, Fari Amini, and Richard Lannon. *A General Theory of Love.* New York: Vintage/Random House, 2000.

Li, Junlei, and Megan M. Julian. "Developmental Relationships as the Active Ingredient: A Unifying Working Hypothesis of 'What Works' across Intervention Settings." *American Journal of Orthopsychiatry* 82, no. 2 (2012): 157–166. https://doi.org/10.1111/j.1939-0025.2012.01151.x.

Lonczak, Heather S., Robert D. Abbott, David Hawkins, Rick Kosterman, and Richard Catalano. "Effects of the Seattle Social Development Project: Behavior, Pregnancy, Birth, and Sexually Transmitted Disease Outcomes by Age 21." *Archives of Pediatric Adolescent Health* 156, no. 5 (2002): 438–47. https://doi.org/10.1001/archpedi.156.5.438.

Long, Nicholas J., Mary M. Wood, and Frank A. Fescer. *Life Space Crisis Intervention: Talking with Students in Conflict.* Austin: Pro-Ed, 2001.

Lopez, Shane J. *Making Hope Happen: Create the Future You Want for Yourself and Others.* New York: Atria, 2013.

Lopez, Shane J. "Hope is a Strategy." YouTube video, 22:01. Posted January 9, 2014. https://www.youtube.com/watch?v=AXBEoTepQHQ.

Lynch, Alicia D., Richard M. Lerner, and Tama Leventhal. "Adolescent Academic Achievement and School Engagement: An Examination of the Role of School-Wide Peer Culture." *Journal of Youth and Adolescence* 42, no.1 (2013): 6–19. https://doi.org/10.1007/s10964-012-9833-0.

MacLean, Paul D. *The Triune Brain in Evolution: Role in Paleocerebral Functions.* New York: Springer, 1990.

Martin, Jennifer, and Carol Stuart. "Working with Cyberspace in the Life-space." *Relational Child and Youth Care Practice* 24, no. 1–2 (2011): 55–66.

Maslow, Abraham H. *A Theory of Human Motivation.* Eastfort: Martino Fine Books, 2013.

Masten, Ann S. *Ordinary Magic: Resilience in Development.* New York: The Guilford Press, 2014.

Masten, Ann S., and Angela J. Narayan. "Child Development in the Context of Disaster, War, and Terrorism: Pathways of Risk and Resilience." *Annual Review of Psychology* 63, no.1 (2012): 227–257. https://dor.org/10.1146/annurev-psych-120710-100356.

McCashen, Wayne. *The Strengths Approach: A Strengths-Based Resource for Sharing Power and Creating Change.* Bendigo: St Luke's Innovative Resources, 2005.

McQuaid, Michelle. "VIA Strengths Mural." Featured Resources. October 16, 2014. http://www.viacharacter.org/resources/via-strengths-mural/.

Meany, Michael J. "Maternal Care, Gene Expression, and Transmission of Individual Differences in Stress Reactivity Across Generations." *Annual Review of Neuroscience* 24 (2001): 1161–92. https://doi.org/10.1146/annurev.neuro.24.1.1161.

Menninger, Karl, Martin Mayman, and Paul Pruyser. *The Vital Balance: The Life Process in Mental Health.* New York: Viking Press, 1963.

MENTOR: The National Mentoring Partnership. *Invest in the Future of America's Children: Support Funding for Mentoring.* 2010. http://www.mentoring.org/downloads/mentoring_1282.pdf.

Messias, DeAnne K. Hilfinger, Elizabeth M Fore, Kerry McLoughlin, and Deborah Parra-Medina. "Adult Roles in Community Programs: Implications for Best Practice." *Family Community Health* 28, no. 3 (2005): 320–37. https://0.1097/00003727-200510000-00005.

Mihalas, Stephanie, William C. Morse, David H. Allsop, and Patricia Alvarez McHatton. "Cultivating Caring Relationships Between Teachers and Secondary Students with Emotional and Behavioral Disorders: Implications for Research and Practice." *Remedial and Special Education* 30, no.2 (2008): 108–25. https://doi.org/10.1177/0741932508315950.

Murphy, John J. *Solution-Focused Counseling in Schools.* Alexandria: American Counseling Organization, 2015.

Murray, Liz. *Breaking Night: A Memoir of Forgiveness, Survival, and My Journey from Homeless to Harvard.* New York: Hyperion, 2010.

Nakazawa, Donna Jackson. *Childhood Disrupted: How Your Biography Becomes Your Biology, and How You Can Heal.* New York: Atria, 2016.

National Resource Center for Permanency and Family Connections. *Placement Stability Information Packet.* US Department of Health and Human Services, Administration for Children and Families, Administration on Children, Youth and Families. Washington, DC. December 2009. http://www.hunter.cuny.edu/socwork/nrcfcpp/info_services/Placement_Stability_Info_Pack.htm.

National Scientific Council on the Developing Child. *Persistent Fear and Anxiety Can Affect Young Children's Learning and Development.* Working paper no. 9. 2010. https://46y5eh11fhgw3ve3ytpwxt9r-wpengine.netdna-ssl.com/wp-content/uploads/2010/05/Persisten t-Fear-and-Anxiety-Can-Affect-Young-Childrens-Learning-and-Development.pdf.

National Scientific Council on the Developing Child. *Supportive Relationships and Active Skill-Building Strengthen the Foundations of Resilience.* Working paper no. 13. 2015. https://46y5eh11fhgw3ve3ytpwxt9r-wpengine.netdna-ssl.com/wp-content/uploads/2015/05/The-Science-of-Resilience2.pdf.

Nelson, Charles A., Nathan A. Fox, and Charles H. Zeanah. "Anguish of the abandoned child." *Scientific American* 308, no 4 (2013): 62–67. https:doi.org/10.1038/scientificamerican0413-62.

Nelson, Charles A., Nathan A. Fox, and Charles H. Zeanah. *Romania's Abandoned Children: Deprivation, Brain Development, and the Struggle for Recovery.* Cambridge: Harvard University Press, 2014.

Neufeld, Gordon, and Gabor Maté. *Hold on to Your Kids: Why Parents Need to Matter More Than Peers.* New York: Ballentine Books, 2014.

Niemiec, Ryan M. *Session 5: A working model.* [Class handout]. VIA intensive Online, The activation of strengths: Bridging research on character strengths into practice: May–June, 2011.

Niemiec, Ryan M. "Mindful Living: Character Strengths Interventions as Pathways for the Five Mindfulness Trainings." *International Journal of Wellbeing* 2, no. 1 (2012): 22–23. https://doi.org/ 10.5502/ijw.v2i1.2.

Niemiec, Ryan M. *Mindfulness and Character Strengths: A Practical Guide to Flourishing.* Ashland: Hogrefe, 2014.

Niemiec, Ryan. "How to Identify VIA Character Strengths: Strength Spotting." Last updated June 26, 2013. http://www.viacharacter.org/blog/how-to-identify-via-character-strengths-to-bring-out-the-best-in-others/.

Niemiec, Ryan M. *Character Strengths Interventions: A Field Guide for Practitioners*. Ashland: Hogrefe, 2017.

Niemiec, Ryan. "A Universal Language That Describes What's Best in Us." YouTube video, 18:58. Posted June 17, 2017. https://www.youtube.com/watch?v=DMWck0mKGWc.

Novembre, Giovanni, Marco Zanon, and Giorgia Silani. "Empathy for Social Exclusion Involves the Sensory-Discriminative Component of Pain: A Within-Subject fMRI Study." *Social Cognitive and Affective Neuroscience* 10, no.2 (2015): 153–164. https://doi.org/10.1093/scan/nsu038.

O'Brien, Rebecca D. "After Harvard, a New Home." *The Harvard Crimson* (April 14, 2003). http://www.thecrimson.com/article/2003/4/14/after-harvard-a-new-home-the/?page=single.

O'Riordan, Colm. "A Forgiving Strategy for the Iterated Prisoner's Dilemma." *Journal of Artificial Societies and Social Simulation* 3, no. 4 (2000). http://jasss.soc.surrey.ac.uk/3/4/3.html.

Ophelia Project, The. "Class Meetings: Creating a Safe School Starting in Your Classroom." The Ophelia Project, 2013. http://www.opheliaproject.org/cass/ClassMeetings.pdf.

Over, Harriet, and Malinda Carpenter. "Eighteen-Month-Old Infants Show Increased Helping Following Priming with Affiliation. *Psychological Science* 20, no. 10 (October 2010): 1189–93. http://dx.doi.org/10.1037/0022-3514.40.1.121.

Panter-Brick, Catherine, and James F. Leckman. "Editorial Commentary: Resilience in Child Development—Interconnected Pathways to Wellbeing." *Journal of Child Psychology and Psychiatry* 54, no. 4 (2013): 333–36. https://doi.org/10.1111/jcpp.12057.

Paper Tigers: One High School's Unlikely Success Story. Produced by KPJR Films. Directed by James Redford. 2015. DVD.

Park, Nannsook, Christopher Peterson, and Martin E. P. Seligman. "Strengths of Character and Well-Being." *Journal of Social and Clinical Psychology* 23, no. 5 (2004): 603–19. https://doi.org/10.1521/jscp.23.5.603.50748.

Perry, Bruce D. "Applying Principles of Neurodevelopment to Clinic Work with Maltreated and Traumatized Children." In *Working with Traumatized Youth in Child Welfare*, edited by Nancy Boyd Webb, 27–52. New York, NY: The Guilford Press, 2006.

Perry, Bruce D., and Erin P. Hambrick. "The Neurosequential Model of Therapeutics." *Reclaiming Children and Youth* 17, no. 3 (Fall 2008): 39–43.

Perry, Bruce. D., and Maia Szalavitz. *The Boy Who Was Raised as A Dog: And Other Stories from a Child Psychiatrist's Notebook—What Traumatized Children Can Teach Us About Loss, Love, and Healing.* New York: Basic Books, 2006.

Perry, Bruce D., Ronnie A. Pollard, Toi L. Blakley, William L. Baker, and Domenico Vigilante. "Childhood Trauma, the Neurobiology of Adaptation, and 'Use-Dependent' Development of the Brain: How 'States' Become 'Traits.'" *Infant Mental Health Journal* 16, no. 4 (Winter 1995): 271–91. https://doi.org/10.1002/1097-0355(199524)16:4<271::AID-IMHJ2280160404>3.0.CO;2-B.

Peterson, Christopher. *A Primer in Positive Psychology*. Oxford: Oxford University Press, 2006.

Peterson, Christopher. "What Is Positive Psychology and What Is It Not?" *Psychology Today* (May 16, 2008). https://www.psychologytoday.com/blog/the-good-life/200805/what-is-positive-psychology-and-what-is-it-not.

Peterson, Christopher, and Martin E. Seligman. *Character Strengths and Virtues: A Handbook and Classification*. Washington, DC: American Psychological Association, 2004.

Pierson, Rita. "Every Kid Needs a Champion." TED video, 7:45. Posted May 2013. https://www.ted.com/talks/rita_pierson_every_kid_needs_a_champion.

Pittman, Karen Johnson, Merita Irby, Joel Tolman, Nicole Yohalem, and Thaddeus Ferber. *Preventing Problems, Promoting Development, Encouraging Engagement: Competing Priorities or Inseparable Goals.* Washington, DC: The Forum for Youth Investment, Impact Strategies, March 2003. https://www.forumfyi.org.

Polly, Shannon, and Kathryn B. Britton. *Character Strengths Matter. How to Live a Full Life.* Positive Psychology News, 2015. Kindle.

Porges, Stephen W. *The Polyvagal Theory: Neurophysiological Foundation of Emotions, Attachment, Communication, and Self-Regulation.* New York: Norton, 2011.

Positive Psychology Institute. "What is positive psychology?". Accessed May 12, 2016. http://www.positivepsychologyinstitute.com.au/what_is_positive_psychology.html.

Press, William H., and Freeman J. Dyson. "Iterated Prisoner's Dilemma Contains Strategies that Dominate any Evolutionary Opponent." *Proceedings of the National Academy of Sciences* 109, no. 26 (2012): 10409–13. https://doi.org/10.1073/pnas.1206569109.

Rashid, Tayyab, and Afroze Anjum. "340 Ways to Use VIA Character Strengths." 2011. Accessed February 8, 2017. https://www.scribd.com/document/312008980/340-Ways-to-Use-Strengths-Tayyab-Rashid.

Rath, Tom, and Mary Reckmeyer. *How Full Is Your Bucket? For Kids.* New York: Gallup Press, 2009.

Ratner, Harvey, and Denise Yusuf. *Brief Counselling with Children and Young People.* New York: Routledge, 2015.

Rah, Soong-Chan. *Many Colors: Cultural Intelligence for a Changing Church*. Chicago: Moody Publishers, 2010. Kindle.

Raychaba, Brian. *Pain ... Lots of Pain: Family Violence and Abuse in the Lives of Young People in Care.* Ottawa: National Youth in Care Network, 1993.

Resilience: The Biology of Stress and the Science of Hope. Produced by KPJR Films. Directed by James Redford. 2016. DVD.

Responsive Classroom. "What is morning meeting?" Posted June 17, 2016. https://www.responsiveclassroom.org/what-is-morning-meeting/.

Rey, Ricardo Arguís. "The Future of Happiness." YouTube video, 15:46. Posted January 16, 2012. www.youtube.com/watch?v=ARcB9KUdv9M.

Rey, Ricardo Arguís, Ana Pilar Bolsas Valero, Silvia Hernández Paniello, and M. del Mar Salvador Monge. *The "Happy Classrooms" Programme: Positive Psychology Applied to Education.* Author, 2014.

https http://educaposit.blogspot.com/p/free-programme-download.html.

Rhodes, Jean E., Belle Liang, and Renee Spencer. "Ethical Issues in Youth Mentoring." In *Handbook of Youth Mentoring,* edited by David L. DuBois and Michael J. Karcher, 511–22. Thousand Oaks: Sage Publications, 2013.

Rhodes-Courter, Ashley. *Three Little Words: A Memoir.* New York: Atheneum, 2008.

Roehlkepartain, Eugene, Kent Pekel, Amy Syvertsen, Jenna Sethi, Theresa Sullivan, and Peter Scales. *Relationships First: Creating Connections that Help Young People Thrive.* Minneapolis: Search Institute, 2017.

Rogoff, Barbara. *Developing Destinies. A Mayan Midwife and Town.* New York, NY: Oxford, 2011. Kindle.

Romens, Sarah E., Jennifer McDonald, John Svaren, and Seth D. Pollak "Associations between Early Life Stress and Gene Methylation in Children." *Child Development* 86, no.1 (Jan–Feb 2015): 303–09. https://doi.org/10.1111/cdev.12270.

Rotter, Julian B. *Social Learning and Clinical Psychology.* Englewood Cliffs: Prentice Hall, 1954.

Saleebey, Dennis. *The Strengths Perspective in Social Work Practice.* Upper Saddle River: Pearson, 2012.

Samdal, Oddrun, Don Nutbeam, Bente Wold, and L. Kannas. "Achieving Health and Educational Goals Through Schools—A Study of the Importance of the School Climate and the Students' Satisfaction with School." *Health Education Research* 13, no. 3 (September 1998): 383–97. https://doi.org/10.1093/her/13.3.383.

Schafer, Dorothy P., Emily K. Lehrman, Amanda G. Kautzman, Ryuta Koyama, Alan R. Mardinly, Ryo Yamasaki, Michael E. Greenberg, Ben A. Barres, and Beth Stevens. "Microglia Sculpt Postnatal Neural Circuits in an Activity and Complement-Dependent Manner." *Neuron* 74, no. 4 (2012): 691–705. https://doi.org/10.1016/j.neuron.2012.03.026.

Schapps, Eric. "The Role of Supportive School Environments in Promoting Academic Success." In *Getting Results, Developing Safe and Healthy Kids Update: Student Health, Supportive Schools, and Academic Success,* 17–52. Developed by the Safe and Healthy Kids Program Office, California Department of Education, 2005. http://cscd.rutgers.edu/file/getresults5_ch3Schaps.pdf.

Schinka, Katherine C., Manfred van Dulmen, Andrea D. Mata, Robert Bossarte, and Monica Swahn. "Psychosocial Predictors and Outcomes of Loneliness Trajectories from Childhood to Early Adolescence." *Journal of Adolescence* 36, no. 6 (December 2013): 1251–60. https://doi.org/10.1016/j.adolescence.2013.08.002.

Schore, Allan N. *Affect Regulation and the Repair of the Self.* New York: Norton, 2003.

Search Institute. "The Power of Relationships in the Lives of Youth." YouTube video, 4:06. Posted August 5, 2017. https://www.youtube.com/watch?v=NPW3ko6GoNE.

Seita, John, and Larry Brendtro. "Reclaiming the Unreclaimable." *Journal of Emotional and Behavioral Problems* 3, no. 4 (1995): 37–41.

Selekman, Matthew D. *Pathways to Change: Brief Therapy Solutions with Difficult Adolescents.* New York, NY: The Guilford Press, 1993.

Seligman, Martin E. P. *Authentic Happiness: Using the New Positive Psychology to Realize Your Potential for Lasting Fulfillment.* New York: Free Press, 2002.

Seligman, Martin E. P. *Flourish: A Visionary New Understanding of Happiness and Well-Being.* New York: Free Press, 2011.

Seligman, Martin. "The New Era of Positive Psychology." TED video, 23:48. Posted 2004. https://www.ted.com/talks/martin_seligman_on_the_state_of_psychology.

Seligman, Martin E. P., and Mihaly Csikszentmihalyi. "Positive Psychology: An Introduction." *American Psychologist* 55, no. 1 (2000): 5–14. http://dx.doi.org/10.1037/0003-066X.55.1.5.

Seligman, Martin E., Randal M. Ernst, Jane Gillham, Karen Reivich, and Mark Linkins. "Positive Education: Positive Psychology and Classroom Interventions." *Oxford Review of Education* 35, no. 3 (2009): 293-311. https://doi.org/ 10.1080/03054980902934563

Seligman, Martin E. P, Tracy A. Steen, Nansook Park, and Christopher Peterson. "Positive Psychology Progress: Empirical Validation of Interventions." *American Psychologist* 60, no. 5 (2005): 410–21. https://doi.org/10.1037/0003-066x.60.5.410.

Senge, Peter. *The Fifth Discipline: The Art & Practice of the Learning Organization*. New York: Doubleday, 1990.

Shirtcliff, Elisabeth A., Christopher L. Coe, and Seth D. Pollak. "Early Childhood Stress Is Associated with Elevated Antibody Levels to Herpes Simplex Virus Type 1." *Proceedings of the National Academy of Sciences* 106, no. 8 (February 2009): 2963–67. https://doi.org/10.1073/pnas.0806660106.

Shonkoff, Jack P., and Deborah A. Phillips. *From Neurons to Neighborhoods: The Science of Early Childhood Development* Washington, DC: National Academic Press, 2000.

Siegel, D. J. *The Developing Mind: How relationships and the brain interact to shape who we are.* New York, NY: Guilford Press, 1999.

Siegel, Daniel J. *Brainstorm: The Power and Purpose of the Teenage Brain.* New York, NY: Penguin, 2013.

Siegel, Daniel J., and Mary Hartzell. *Parenting from the Inside Out: How a Deeper Self-Understanding Can Help You Raise Children Who Thrive.* Los Angeles: J. P. Tarcher, 2003.

Six Dimensions of National Culture. The Hofstede Insights. Accessed November 3, 2016. https://www.hofstede-insights.com/models/national-culture/.

Slaby, Andrew, and Lili Frank Garfinkel. *No One Saw My Pain: Why Teens Kill Themselves.* New York: W. W. Norton, 1994.

Smith, Emily Esfahani. *The Power of Meaning: Crafting a Life That Matters.* New York: Crown, 2017.

Smith, Sean M., and Wylie W. Vale. "The Role of the Hypothalamic-Adrenal Axis in Neuroendocrine Responses to Stress." *Dialogues Clinical Neuroscience* 8, no. 4 (February 2006): 383–95. https://www.ncbi.nlm.nih.gov/pmc/articles/PMC3181830/.

Snyder, M., J. Riese, S. P. Limber, & N. Mullin. *Class Meetings That Matter: A Year's Worth of Resources for Grades 9–12.* Center City, MN: Hazelden, 2012. Accessed from https://www.hazelden.org/HAZ_MEDIA/3981_ClassMeetingsThatMatter.pdf.

Sousa, David A. *How the Brain Learns.* Thousand Oaks: Corwin, 2015.

Spitz, René A. "Anaclitic Depression." In *The Psychoanalytic Study of the Child*, edited by R. S. Eisller. New York: International Universities Press, 1946.

Steinberg, Lawrence. *Age of Opportunity: Lessons from the Science of Adolescence.* Boston: Mariner Books, 2014.

Tough, Paul. *Helping Children Succeed: What Works and Why.* New York, NY: Houghton Mifflin Harcourt, 2016.

Turneya, Kristin, and Christopher Wildeman. "Adverse Childhood Experiences among Children Placed In and Adopted from Foster Care: Evidence from a Nationally Representative Survey." *Child Abuse and Neglect* 64 (February 2017): 117–29. https://doi.org/10.1016/j.chiabu.2016.12.009.

Tutu, Desmond. *No Future Without Forgiveness.* New York: Doubleday, 1999.

UM News Service. "Christopher Peterson: What Makes Life Worth Living? (Part 1)" YouTube video, 4:30. Posted October 18 2011. https://www.youtube.com/watch?v=DRiIAqGXLKA.

UM News Service. "Christopher Peterson: What Makes Life Worth Living? (Part 2)." YouTube Video, 3:49. Posted October 18, 2011. https://www.youtube.com/watch?v=SvZQsqHVjHU.

US Department of Education. *Promoting Grit, Tenacity, and Perseverance: Critical Factors in the 21st Century.* US Department of Education,

Office of Educational Technology, February 2013. http://pgbovine.net/OET-Draft-Grit-Report-2-17-13.pdf.

van der Kolk, Bessel. "The Neurobiology of Childhood Trauma and Abuse." *Child and Adolescent Psychiatric Clinical of North America* 12, no. 2 (2003): 293–327. https://doi.org/10.1016/S1056-4993(03)00003-8.

van der Kolk, Bessel. *The Body Keeps the Score: Brain, Mind, and Body in the Healing of Trauma.* New York: Penguin, 2014.

Veenstra, René, Jan Kornelis Dijkstra, Christian Steglich, and Maarten H. W. Van Zalk. "Network-Behavior Dynamics." *Journal of Research on Adolescence* 23, no. 3 (2013): 399–412. https://doi.org/10.1111/jora.12070.

Vernon, Rachael, and Elaine Papps. "Cultural Safety and Continuing Competence." In *Cultural Safety in Aotearoa New Zealand,* edited by Dianne Wepa, 51–64. Port Melbourne: Cambridge University, 2015.

VIA Institute on Character. *VIA Survey.* Accessed January 5, 2018. https://www.viacharacter.org/survey/account/register.

VIA Character Strengths Blog (n.d.). Accessed from http://www.viacharacter.org/blog/.

VIA Institute on Character. "Positive Education with Character Strengths." YouTube video, 8:36. Posted April 12, 2011. https://www.youtube.com/watch?v=wZYveRLtXXY&index=12&list=PLgncVU3SDSCkNroPV7HUhQiipk_FDgnvi.

VIA Institute on Character. "VIA PRO Character Strengths Profile." Accessed January 3, 2018. https://www.viacharacter.org/www/Portals/0/VIA%20Pro%20Report.pdf.

von Dawans, Bernadette, Urs Fischbacher, Clemens Kirschbaum, Ernst Fehr, and Markus Heinrichs. "The Social Dimension of Stress Reactivity: Acute Stress Increases Prosocial Behavior in

Humans." *Psychological Science* 23, no. 7 (2012): 651–60. https://doi.org/10.1177/0956797611431576.

Walter, Joanna. "Liz Murray: My Parents Were Desperate Drug Addicts. I'm a Harvard Graduate." *The Guardian* (September 25, 2010). https://www.theguardian.com/world/2010/sep/26/liz-murray-bronx-harvard.

Warneken, Felix, and Michael Tomasello. "Altruistic Helping in Human Infants and Young Chimpanzees." *Science* 311 (March 3, 2006): 1301–03. https://doi.org/10.1111/j.1467-9280.2009.02419.x.

Wentzel, Kathryn R. "Social Relationships and Motivation in Middle School." *Journal of Educational Psychology* 90, no. 2 (1998): 202–209. https://doi.org/10.1037/0022-0663.90.2.202.

Wepa, Dianne. "Culture and Ethnicity: What is the Question?" In *Cultural Safety in Aotearoa New Zealand*, edited by Dianne Wepa, 65–78. Port Melbourne: Australia: Cambridge University Press.

Werner, Emmy E., and Ruth S. Smith. *Overcoming the Odds: High Risk Children from Birth to Adulthood.* Ithaca: Cornell University Press, 1992.

White, Michael. "The externalization of the problem and the re-authoring of lives and relationships." *Dulwich Centre Newsletter* (1969): 3–21.

White, Michael, and David Epston. *Narrative Ways to Therapeutic Ends.* New York: Norton, 1990.

Whitlock, Janis L. "Youth Perceptions of Life at School: Contextual Correlates of School Connectedness in Adolescence." *Applied Developmental Science* 10, no 1 (2010): 13–29. https://10.1207/s1532480xads1001_2.

Wilkins, Sheri, and Carol Burmeister. *FLIPP the Switch: Strengthen Executive Function Skills.* Lenaxa: Autism Asperger Publishing, 2015.

Wilson, Dorian. "The Interface of School Climate and School Connectedness and Relationships with Aggression and Victimization." *Journal of School Health* 74, no. 7 (2004): 293–99. https://doi.org/10.1111/j.1746-1561.2004.tb08286.x.

Wolin, Steven, and Sybil Wolin. *Survivor's Pride: Introduction to Resiliency* [DVD]. United States: Attainment Company, 2012.

Wong, Paul T. P., Lilian C. J. Wong, Marvin J. McDonald, and Derrick W. Klaassen. *The Positive Psychology of Meaning and Spirituality: Selected Papers from Meaning Conferences*. Birmingham: Purpose Research, 2012.

Made in the
USA
Middletown, DE